The **Ministry** of **Leadership**
Heart and Theory

· · · · ·

Glenn Terrell, Ph.D.

PACIFIC
INSTITUTE
PUBLISHING

Pacific Institute Publishing
1709 Harbor Avenue SW • Seattle, Washington 98126-2049
(206) 628-4800 • www.thepacificinstitute.com
Editorial: Christy A. Watson
Design/Production: Courtney Cook Hopp
Printed in Canada by Friesens Corp.

ISBN 1-930622-01-5

I dedicate this book to my family, including my wife, Gail,
who provided encouragement, love, support and suggestions;
my children, Francie and Glenn for their love and understanding
of the heavy demands of the presidency when they were growing up
in Pullman; and my charming and witty grandchildren,
Michael and Andy.

"Dr. Terrell's deep reflection on his years as President of Washington State University provides valuable advice on how to create an ideal vision and how to grow from controversy. It is an indispensable guide for heart, soul and mind, for interior disposition and exterior relationships, and for how to 'do things right' and 'do the right thing.' Leaders of all organizations will benefit from it."
—ROBERT J. SPITZER, S.J., PH.D.
President, Gonzaga University

"Glenn Terrell was the right person for Washington State University at a time which was right for him. He served brilliantly during the time of student troubles in the 1960s and early 70s, and this account of his presidency is both informative and a good read."
—JIM SHORT, PH.D.
Professor Emeritus of Sociology

"If you do not already know Glenn Terrell personally, you will after you have read this account of his tenure as president of Washington State University. Those of us who have had the privilege of knowing him, and especially those of us fortunate enough to have worked with him, know that his mind has always been in close touch with his heart, the principle theme of this delightful yet instructive book. His warmth, sincerity, wonderful sense of humor and, most of all, his unquenchable love for students and their school — the latter an attribute far too few of today's college presidents possess — are evident on every page. Glenn is my model for the educational leader who knows how to blend intellect, common sense and fun into a mixture for success and effectiveness. You will find from reading *The Ministry of Leadership* that you will draw the same inescapable conclusion."
—JOHN SLAUGHTER, PH.D.
President & CEO, National Action Council for Minorities in Engineering

MESSAGE FROM THE PUBLISHER

Having worked with Washington State University's football team in the 1970s, I knew Glenn Terrell to be an exceptional college president and an effective leader. I saw wisdom in Glenn from his presidency and Diane and I knew that what he had to offer would make a significant difference, not only to Diane and myself, but to all those coming into The Pacific Institute. We were right.

In addition to his proven leadership skills, Diane and I recognized Glenn's reputation in the field of psychology. We have relied on him to keep us up-to-date on the latest research in the cognitive sciences, as well as keep us in contact with those preeminent psychologists whose research forms the foundations of our programs. Glenn's quarterly publication, *The LETTER*, allows us to provide this information to our clients and associates around the world.

On any given day, you will find staff members and Institute associates in Glenn's office, all seeking the benefit of his knowledge, experience and wisdom. Each leaves his presence with considerable information, highlighted with personal stories and the benefit of a lifetime of learning.

Glenn's wisdom has assisted many of us in our decision-making, which is why Diane and I felt it was time for him to share it with everybody. So, we encouraged Glenn to write this book – the first of several. I feel confident that his wisdom and knowledge will provide some powerful insights that will guide your future, just as it has mine.

—LOU TICE, CHAIRMAN
The Pacific Institute, Inc.

ACKNOWLEDGMENTS

First, I want to express my appreciation to Lou and Diane for wanting to publish this book and for their unflagging support throughout the preparation of the manuscript.

I am honored that the following distinguished colleagues read the manuscript and offered important suggestions: Governor and United States Senator from Washington State, Dan Evans; WSU President, Lane Rawlins; President Lois DeFleur, Binghamton University, State University New York; John Slaughter, former Provost, WSU, President University of Maryland and Occidental College, Director of the National Science Foundation and currently President of the National Action Council for Minorities in Engineering, Inc.; Father Bob Spitzer, President of Gonzaga University; professors Jim Short, WSU and Albert Bandura, Jordan Chair in Psychology, Stanford University.

Three colleagues at The Pacific Institute have worked tirelessly, on weekends and at work, to prepare the manuscript for publication: Christy Watson has edited and proofread the work in her usual conscientious and thorough manner; Ron Schau provided the very important computer expertise; and Courtney Cook Hopp has done a creative job with the design and art work. These three, in addition to their creativity and hard work, have been personally "into" their work on the manuscript, on what has turned out to be a fast track for early publication. I cannot thank them enough for their actual help and for their helpful attitudes.

At WSU, the following friends and colleagues have provided absolutely essential assistance in various ways. Sue Hinz, Tim Marsh, Bob Hilliard, News Bureau; Sharon Morgan, WSU Foundation; Bob Smalley, Alumni Association; Karen Fisher, President's Office; Steve Nakata, Multicultural Affairs; Dawn Thompson, Student Affairs; Gen DeVleming, former assistant to the president; Linda Glover, Provost Office; and Cathy Fulkerson, Institutional Research. My thanks to all of you for providing the very important information.

My thanks to Mark Ufkes, Lynn Claudon, Paul Casey and Mike Bernard for urging me to write the book and for offering helpful suggestions after reading the manuscript.

I appreciate the thoughtful email messages encouraging me to share the wisdom acquired during my eighteen year tenure as president of WSU.

Last but not least, I thank the faculty, students and alumni of WSU for permitting me to serve their needs for eighteen years, and for many of the most cherished memories of my life.

TABLE OF CONTENTS

FOREWORD

I read Glenn Terrell's manuscript with great interest because I also lived through many of those experiences as a faculty member. Glenn's accounts are instructive as well as accurate, vivid and entertaining. Most of all, I appreciated the Glenn Terrell I have always known: learning from each new experience, using each challenge as an opportunity to teach others, and giving nearly everyone the benefit of the doubt.

Anyone who loves Washington State University will find this book irresistible. Others interested in administration or leadership will be impressed with the countless examples of courage, forbearance and vision. At the heart of the book and in the heart of this particular leader, you find a lot of insight and wisdom.

Having been there, I marvel at Glenn's objective view of personal attacks on his character, his charity towards many who were not charitable to him, and his accounting of the lessons learned.

This is a record of a truly remarkable time for WSU, the nation and the world. Glenn led with his heart and made a lasting impression on a university that is better for what he gave. I think so highly of the work that it will have an honored place on my shelf, just next to the work of Enoch A. Bryan.

—V. Lane Rawlins, President
Washington State University

INTRODUCTION

A number of years ago, a conference was held at the Wingspread Conference Center in Wisconsin, involving university presidents and chancellors who had successfully survived the student activism period of the mid-1960s and early-1970s. The Wingspread Conference Center, designed by Frank Lloyd Wright and supported by the Johnson Wax Company, assembles participants who are authorities in various topics of current significance and interest. Examples are initiatives in economic, educational, international and social issues. The purpose of this meeting was to encourage participants to prepare a document of their experiences that would be helpful to future leaders in higher education who have the "privilege" of presiding over periods of extreme unrest. I use the word privilege for a very good reason: Some very productive changes have been made in the way universities govern themselves as a result of the excesses of some students and faculties during this period in American higher education history. But more about that later.

The attendees at the Wingspread Conference, held in 1985, were some of America's most distinguished university leaders. I was honored to be included with the following:

- Bill Boyd, former President of the University of Oregon and President of the Field Museum
- Laurence Chalmers, former President of the University of Kansas and President of the Art Institute in Chicago
- Robben Fleming, former President of the University of Michigan
- The Reverend Ted Hesburgh, President of the University of Notre Dame
- James Hester, President of New York Botanical Gardens
- Roger Heyns, Chancellor, University of California, Berkeley, and President of the Hewlett Foundation
- Grayson Kirk, President of Columbia University
- Bill McGill, Chancellor, University of California, San Diego, and President of Columbia University
- John Oswald, President, Pennsylvania State University
- James Perkins, President, Cornell University
- Martha Peterson, President of Barnard and Beloit Colleges
- Nathan Pusey, President of Harvard University
- Edwin Young, President, University of Wisconsin, Madison.

Responding to the Wingspread conference is important. To my knowledge, there has been only one book written on student activism by any of the attendees, *The Year of the Monkey,* by William McGill. It is a well-written account of student activism at the University of California at San Diego, where McGill was chancellor in 1968 and 1969.

There are also other reasons for writing this book. Only one Washington State University President, Enoch Bryan, has recorded his experiences and a part of those of his successor, President Holland. WSU, its students, faculty, alumni and regents are the main forces that impelled me to write about some of the important events and experiences of my eighteen years as their president.

Also, a number colleagues, friends, former students, and others have been gently applying pressure to write the book. Some have come not so gently with such saucy statements as, "You are not getting any younger," and "You are not going to live forever." One alumna urged me to get going on the book, "while you can still remember what happened." My friends and employers, the founders of The Pacific Institute, Lou and Diane Tice, have provided encouragement and support.

I have more to share than the unrest era. I became interested in how decisions were made in colleges and universities during my eighteen-year tenure, which covered significant parts of three decades. I had not been in the president's role long before it was obvious to me that presidents essentially are decision-makers. I became a student of the processes involved in making decisions in higher education, and how important it is to understand the vital relationship between institutional goals and many of those decisions. Also, I quickly learned the importance of the involvement of the constituents on and off campus, particularly those whose professional and personal lives would be affected by decisions.

It disturbs me that many decisions in higher education are driven primarily by the pressures of constituent groups rather than from a well-conceived idea, theory, vision or conceptual framework of how a university can best serve the people who created the idea of a university hundreds of years ago. The temptations are strong to make decisions that will not alienate a particular constituency, or will please the largest number, or the most powerful constituents. This is not to say that the effect of decisions on the various groups that comprise the university should not be carefully analyzed before decisions are made, particularly with respect to the lives of those affected by the decision. Not to do so would be, at the least, inconsiderate and at most both inconsiderate and unwise. And, in some instances, it would be heartless.

I acknowledge the influence of Michael Cohen and James March on my thinking. These men wrote a book on university leadership, for one of the eighty or so titles of the Carnegie Commission on Higher Education, on the need for university leaders to develop a conceptual framework and organizational theory, including a well-articulated vision which would give some consistency in decision-making. March and Cohen decried the failure of university scholars to study organizational theory of universities, while focusing heavily on scholarly research in corporations and public agencies. I'm afraid that the resistance on the part of universities to analyze their own organizations still exists.

It seems appropriate to include in the introduction an important part of my life far from the halls of academe, but related later to my decision to enter the educational world – my three plus years of military service during World War II. On Sunday afternoon, December 7, 1941 I was studying (an all too infrequent activity for me in those carefree undergraduate years) in my dormitory room at Davidson College, North Carolina when the news of the Japanese attack on Pearl Harbor came on my radio. In very grave tones, President Roosevelt informed the American people of the attack. His voice was characteristically strong and his words reassuring.

This was both scary and comforting to a 21 year old college senior enrolled in the advanced Army ROTC program. I was scheduled to receive both a BA degree in Political Science and a 2nd Lieutenant's commission in five months. I was ripe for the plucking for military service. The following June found me at Fort Benning, Georgia, the Army's training ground. I was enrolled in what I thought was a program for company commanders. It turned out to be for platoon leaders who some day *hoped* to become company commanders.

My next assignment was as a platoon leader with the 30th Infantry Division in Camp Blanding, Florida. After helping to put division recruits through basic training, I was transferred to the Headquarters Company of the 7th Corps, preparing for the invasion on D-Day, June 6, 1944. I hit Utah Beach with the 7th Corps on June 6th. My assignment with the 7th Corps continued until the end of World War II.

My interest in teaching as a career came while I was giving training instruction to the recruits in the 30th Infantry Division and the members of the 7th Corps, Headquarters Company. The Commanding General of the 7th Corps, a Lieutenant General, happened to observe one of my instructional sessions. He liked what he observed and later requested that I give him a refresher course in weapons of the infantry, which of course I did. The General then requested that I be promoted to 1st Lieutenant. To any-one familiar with the military, you will not be surprised to learn that the promotion was promptly processed. The General's recognition of my teaching ability was extraordinarily rewarding.

I found that the almost four years of service to my country helped generate in me a strong sense of pride rather than resentment, a marvelous feeling that I have carried with me in my teaching, research and administrative careers. Events since September 11, 2001 and the allegations of fraud on the part of some of our most successful corporate executives have intensified my feeling of loyalty to our nation.

After three and a half years of unsuccessful experience in law school and the insurance business, I found fulfillment and success in education. My career in education includes assignments at five universities, including Florida State University, in my hometown of Tallahassee, Florida. It was there that I received my Masters degree in Psychology, and spent five years as an instructor and Assistant Professor on the faculty of the Department of Psychology. At the University of Iowa, I received my Doctorate in Developmental Psychology. I was at the University of Colorado for eight years, where I was the Chair of the Department of Psychology for two of those years. At the University of Illinois - Chicago, I served as Dean of the College of Liberal Arts and Dean of Faculties for two years each. And, finally, my eighteen year tenure as the President of Washington State University.

This book will include a chapter on the reflections of life after the presidency, a very important phase for someone who has given heart, love and 24-hour days for eighteen years in the service of an excellent university. For fifteen years as I write today, the middle of June, 2002, I have had the very challenging assignment as an educational advisor to The Pacific Institute, an educational company with offices in several countries whose headquarters is in Seattle. Founded in 1971 by Lou and Diane Tice, The Pacific Institute provides services to all kinds of organizations, designed to help their employees perform better than they have ever experienced. Most of the concepts used in our seminars, programs and consulting services are central to social cognitive psychological theory developed largely by Albert Bandura of Stanford University, and explanatory style of Martin Seligman at the University of Pennsylvania, their students and other devotees.

So, I am back where I started my academic career 50 years ago. Working with the Tices and others at The Pacific Institute has enabled me to continue my personal development as well as provide assistance to the company. Some university presidents want to play golf (most of them poorly), fish and travel when they retire. Not this former president. I want to continue to be productive as long as I am able to do so.

The last chapter of this book will include more about the value of the work of The Pacific Institute, because of its emphasis on optimal individual and organizational development. Although we work with all kinds of organizations, one of the main initiatives of the Institute involves work with K through 12 educational systems.

Three books were published in 1990 in connection with the centennial celebration of WSU. They are well-written histories of the development of WSU from the early years in the 1890s to 1990. One is on general history, written by Professor George Frykman of the WSU History department; Another is about Cougar sports, by Richard Fry of the WSU news service; and the third is by William Stimson, on student life. Reference information about these and other books and journal articles appears in the Bibliography. I recommend that everyone interested in WSU add these books to their library, if you have not already done so. This book, however, like President Bryan's earlier book, is written from the president's perspective. Understandably, it will be different from the others in some ways. Hopefully, it contains useful information for someone who wants to know more about how one of WSU's presidents perceives events that occurred during his tenure, as well as his general views of the leadership role of the president in defining and shaping the university.

Some significant events occurred during my watch, from 1967 to 1985, a period, as I mentioned earlier, that encompasses major parts of three decades. The goal is not to simply list the events, but to examine what they meant in the life of the university, and to present an analysis of the theoretical and practical variables that entered into the decisions as to how these events were managed. Also, effort will be directed toward expanding some of the views that Cohen, March, and others have long held to be important. Finally, I will show how effective leadership of a university, theoretically impossible to accomplish, can indeed be accomplished, but only with the cooperation of dedicated regents, faculty, students, alumni and administrative colleagues. It would be impossible for me to over-emphasize the importance of their help.

Before proceeding to Chapter One, I would like to explain the major factor that helped me to decide which events to include in this book, among all the experiences that occurred during my tenure. Most of the situations that arise in the life of a university president are both interesting and important. I had to make a decision about which events were the most important to the central theme of this book, as conveyed by the title, *The Ministry of Leadership*, as well as the importance of the leader's decisions reflecting his/her theory of a university and the goals of the institution. And, if I occasionally digress from my main points, I hope you will indulge me. After all, a lot goes on in eighteen years.

Chapter One

ABOUT THE TITLE OF THE BOOK

Much research literature on leadership focuses on the traits essential for successful leadership, or the traits that distinguish successful from unsuccessful leaders. Vision and Integrity are on most lists; Energy and Courage are less frequently mentioned. Heart rarely, if ever, is mentioned, at least not in terms of the definition of Heart I use. What does Heart mean? It is difficult to define, but not difficult to recognize. And some may say its importance may vary with the institution. Maybe so. At any rate, at Washington State University between 1967 and 1985, I considered it an essential trait. Heart is not cognitive in nature, like vision and creativity. Rather it is emotional, like love and intense compassion, indicating *profound personal commitment.*

Although I have not discussed this with him, this definition of Heart is similar to what Father Bob Spitzer, President of Gonzaga University, would refer to as Happiness Level III. Here, the purpose of an individual driven by his/her heart is directed toward the welfare of others and the organization. Father Bob Spitzer, former WSU President, Enoch Bryan, and President Lane Rawlins are examples of those functioning at Level III as leaders. Abraham Lincoln is an obvious historical example. In the history of the state of Washington, I include former U. S. Senator and Washington State Governor Dan Evans; many Washington State University professors, including professors emeritus Herbert Eastlick and Jim Short; Wallis Beasley, Interim President and Executive Vice President; Academic Vice President John Slaughter; alumni Phil Lighty, Weldon "Hoot" Gibson, Art and Helen Brunstad, and Harold and Jean Olsen. All are excellent examples. There are numerous others, of course. In fact, I could name dozens of others – regents, alumni, administrators and faculty. But the meaning of Heart, as an important trait of leaders, is certainly exemplified in the character and performance of the few leaders listed above. They gave, and continue to give, of themselves unsparingly.

This book's title, *The Ministry of Leadership*, is important to me, personally, for the following reason. During my adolescent years and early twenties, I seriously considered the ministry, a member of the clergy, as a career. But I never quite believed that I was called or "supposed" to do so. When I joined the world of higher education, I quickly recognized that as a faculty member I was ministering to the educational needs of students and faculty. In each administrative position – department chair, dean and president – the need for ministering, or providing care for members of the university community, increased. Leading a university through the hysteria of campus demonstrations or the paralyzing fear created by the explosion of Mt. St. Helens, and the repeated disappointments of legislative appropriations — plus a host of other experiences common to many higher education leaders, big-city Mayors and governors — require ministering skills of the highest order.

Often it is difficult to relate the content of a book to the title. Not so in this book. My main purpose in writing this book is to explain how important I believe the concepts of Heart and Ministry were to whatever success I was able achieve as president of WSU. I believe they are the traits that were necessary for me to enjoy excellent relationships with the students, alumni, legislators and regents. And they were the traits that, combined with my high academic standards and my goal of enhancing the research and graduate programs, enabled me to enjoy the respect of many of the faculty leaders.

The importance of theory in the title springs from Cohen and March's theme as expressed in the introduction. Occasional references to the components of organizational theory will be made throughout this book in explanations of the relationships between theory, priorities and goals in presidential decisions.

Let me hasten to add that Vision, Integrity, Courage and Energy are givens. Without them a university president cannot and should not survive. The following discussion, centering on these four "givens" reflects the views of some of the leading researchers and authors of books and journal articles, as well as some of my own. My belief in the preeminence of the Heart of a university leader, as I have defined it, is expressed throughout the book in many ways, particularly through the descriptions of relationships with students, faculty, alumni and the people of the State of Washington.

Vision

Vision is important because it is the institution's compass, the goals that are established as a result of a planning process that involves shared governance: governing board, administrators, faculty, staff and students, both current and former. John Gardner, former Secretary of Health, Education and Welfare in Lyndon Johnson's administration and a highly respected public servant and leader, wrote that two main tasks of the leader are "goal-setting and motivating." Goal-setting is an important cognitive skill designed to identify the vision of the organization. Gardner, who also founded Common Cause and the Urban League, further elaborates on his views of the task of the leader as a "process of persuasion . . . by which the leader induces a group to pursue objectives held by the leader or shared by the leader and his followers." Presumably, Gardner means that the objectives are arrived at by goal-setting, an important skill central to The Pacific Institute's success in working with clients. Dr. Donald Kennedy, Editor of *Science*, the publication of the American Association for the Advancement of Science, stated in a recent editorial obituary that Dr. Gardner once said that, "the first and last task of the leader is to keep hope alive."

The president's vision for the institution is an exceedingly important piece in the process of formulating and articulating the organization's mission, and for the allocation of resources in a manner consistent with the vision. As mentioned in the introduction, the president's essential job is to make decisions, and the most important decisions are those related to institutional goals. Putting it another way, the goals of the institution are what the organization stands for, what it's suppose to be doing, its organizational theory.

Scholars of leadership research such as James Burns and Bernard Bass, K. E. Clark and M. B. Clark, have distinguished transactional from transformational leadership. These are interesting concepts that have received much attention in the voluminous literature on leadership. The former is usually equated to the more routine management responsibilities, while the latter to the more "charismatic" role of the leader, as in vision-building and decision-making. The Clarks, as the title of their book suggests (*Choosing to Lead*), emphasize that leadership is something that originates with a decision by the person who decides that she/he wants to lead. The Clarks then identify the traits that make the leaders successful and the kinds of programs that will enhance leadership development. I consider their approach to be an important contribution to the literature.

Integrity

The tragic investment losses suffered by many Americans, apparently created by the lack of integrity among some of America's corporate leaders, underscores the importance of honesty on the part of our chosen leaders. Higher education is not without examples of fraudulent behavior. Warren Bennis, in this author's opinion the nation's top researcher in leadership, consistently reports that trust is one of the most frequently mentioned traits by respondents in his interviews with distinguished corporate, education and government leaders.

Simple, old-fashioned honesty consistently is judged to be essential in leaders. Admittedly, some members of the university community occasionally judge disagreement as a lack of trust. I observed this phenomenon quite frequently during the emotional campus unrest days. Also, sometimes it becomes necessary to postpone or even reverse agreed-upon decisions because of unexpected events that are beyond the control of the leader. For example, legislative action may make funding a decision about a new program impossible. One of the best ways leaders can be sincere is to make every possible effort to do what they say they are going to do about such things as appointments, and above all, about the legal use of appropriated or donated funds. Occasionally, we have seen violations of the latter type. This offense by one university leader or an association can give all universities a bad image, especially if the allocation of federal, state or donated funds are in question.

Courage

A university president faces daily issues that require courage, especially if the president believes in the preeminence of the heart in her/his duties as president. Decisions usually make some constituents angry, disappointed or sad. It is essential that the leader make decisions that he/she believes to be in the best interest of the university over-all. The president must believe that the general welfare of the university transcends the interest of any individual or group of individuals within the university.

The meaning of heart and ministry, as I use it, must relate to the profound personal commitment to the university as a whole, not any particular group, especially when applied to decisions flowing from the goals of the institution. Heart and ministry also demand that the leader, if possible, take action directed toward making those disaffected by a decision continue to believe that they are important to the university. In retrospect, I probably did not do enough of the things that would have encouraged those faculty members who were recruited primarily to teach, to feel that they continued to be important to the university.

Energy

There is no question about it, the presidency requires boundless energy. If the president is approachable and lives on campus, he/she is on 24-hour duty. Many of the readers of this book will remember that the WSU president's residence is on campus. I would not have it any other way. In fact, when I began my tenure in the summer of 1967, the Regents gave me the choice of living in the existing residence, constructed in 1915, or a new home off-campus. Of course, in Pullman, living off-campus would still be close to campus and everything else. Furthermore, asking for funds to build a new president's home in my first budget presentation to the legislature did not exactly thrill me.

My devotion to Washington State University was boundless. My heart was in that university (and still is) big time. That fact alone increased energy demands. Needless to say, I chose the existing residence on Campus Avenue. Every day seemed like open house, which was usually great fun, and always interesting, even during campus activism when 3,000 students came to the president's house demanding that I end the war in Vietnam as well as end racism throughout the world.

With bull horn in hand, I told them that if I didn't love them, I would be afraid. Actually, I *was* just a little nervous, particularly about what I was going to say. But I had a genuine fondness for them, nevertheless. I told them that I would like nothing better than to end that unpopular war and to end racism world-wide. Much to the disappointment of a handful of students, who felt that I had not promised them that I would do exactly as they demanded, the rest of them disappeared quietly into the night, seemingly satisfied that they had made their case. I had agreed with their belief that war and racism are grossly evil, horrible and unfair.

Back to the energy requirement. My schedule included only about five hours average sleep per night for years. Fortunately, I come from pioneer stock. My father moved from Mississippi to Florida in a covered wagon 125 years ago. He later spent 40 years on the Florida Supreme Court bench. I learned much from him about ethics and hard work.

Chapter Two

THE EARLY YEARS

I n late fall of 1965, I received a letter from the regents of Washington State University inquiring of my interest in the presidency. At the time, I was deeply involved in the development of the new campus of the University of Illinois-Chicago, as dean of the College of Arts and Sciences. This factor led me to decline such inquiries, at least until I felt that I had accomplished as much as I intended when I started at UI-Chicago in 1963. Also, I was conflicted as to whether or not I wanted to be a university president. However, the regents made the presidency of Washington State University so attractive, I was tempted enough to agree to visit the campus in Pullman.

The visit was both interesting and enjoyable. I liked the people and the way they talked about their university. I also liked the fact that they included faculty, students, alumni, the retiring president, Clement French, as well as the regents in the meetings. This told me that there was a genuine commitment to shared governance on campus, a principle that appealed to me. The very visible commitment to the value of higher education on the part of the people in the State of Washington also helped.

The Board of Regents reached a decision promptly. Two weeks

after my visit, I received a telephone call, offering me the presidency. After a week or so of self-examination, I declined their offer. A combination of my equivocating about the presidency and the short time I had been at the University of Illinois led me to believe that it was better for Washington State University and me not to accept their offer. The decision to decline the offer in no way meant that I was disappointed with what I had learned about their university. In fact, I decided that if I ever resolved my uncertainty about undertaking the heavy responsibilities of a presidency, I would like it to be at Washington State University. Further, I enjoyed the teaching and research more than I thought I might enjoy the nature of the president's responsibilities, which seemed too far removed from the main mission of a university – teaching and research. I must confess that the remote location of WSU was a factor, not a controlling one obviously, but one that might have made recruiting and retaining faculty difficult. It did not take long for me to realize that location was one of the important *assets* of WSU.

After hearing my reasons for declining their offer, the regents at Washington State University invited me to make another trip to the campus for further conversations. Despite my response to their offer, they persuaded me to visit the campus again. I boarded a flight to Spokane at O'Hare airport, and immediately came to the conclusion that the probability of my accepting their offer was not high enough to justify my consuming more of their time and money. I bounded off the plane and headed home, feeling good about my decision.

The conflict, so clear in my behavior, is a classic example of approach-avoidance conflict. When we have two goals of approximately equal attractiveness, we will often vacillate between the two goals. The closer we move towards one goal, the more attractive the other goal becomes. The WSU goal was so attractive that I had to actually board the plane to come to a decision. The fact that I felt great about my decision indicates resolution of the conflict. Fortunately, I had another opportunity to go to WSU.

Actually, there was more involved than my uncertainty about becoming a university president. I refer to the ethical implications of using an offer from one institution to improve one's conditions of employment in another. To me, that is at least misleading and deceptive, and some would say a form of dishonesty. And yet, I know that competing with other institutions for high quality faculty and students is necessary if our goal is to improve the quality of our institutions of higher education. The best, admittedly partial, solution for this problem is for leaders to keep accurate data about market values in the academic world, and to make every effort to have salaries and benefits reflect these values. Theoretically at least, we price our most productive faculty out of the market, so they will not be flirting around with other universities, looking for offers.

About eight months later I received a call from the president of the Board of Regents at Washington State University asking me if I would reconsider my decision. The additional time at the University of Illinois combined with the worst snowstorm in Chicago's history, persuaded me to say "yes." Another six months found my family and me in Pullman, Washington. I never regretted my decision. At the same time, I frequently wondered how long I wanted to remain as president, not because I wasn't challenged by the position, but because many of the duties of the office took me away from the original reason for entering higher education, teaching and research, both of which involve students and faculty.

My first six months were spent mostly in getting acquainted with my colleagues on and off campus. I decided to refrain from any comments about my specific goals for the university until I had time to get a grasp of the culture at Washington State University, a period I estimated to be six months. As I should have realized, that quiet period turned out to be closer to six weeks than six months. It was important that my general vision for the future of WSU be made known, which I repeat here.

In a general sense, I saw two goals: 1) a continued improvement in the quality of the total undergraduate experience, academic and social, and 2) the expansion and strengthening of the graduate programs and research. I vividly remember the pressure to be more specific, such as which undergraduate and graduate programs. It is very important to me that I make clear that I held steadfastly to these two goals for the duration of my tenure. I was convinced then that there was something precious about the feelings that former and currently enrolled students had about their university, a feeling of loyalty much stronger than I had observed in any of my other colleges and universities. This includes Davidson College, an excellent liberal arts college and my undergraduate school of only six hundred students. My determination to maintain that sense of pride and loyalty of the undergraduate student body was strong and ever-present in my thinking, as was my determination to see WSU become one of the top 25 most distinguished public research universities in the nation. My ultimate goal was to have WSU admitted to the prestigious Association of American Universities.

In the early fall of 1967, four months after my arrival, we set in motion a system designed to enlist the cooperation of faculty, student and staff groups to participate in more specific ways in the development of a vision for the future of WSU. With the assistance of Academic Vice President Wallis Beasley, Graduate School Dean Jim Short, faculty and student leaders, we created Study Councils for all major academic and non-academic groups. These groups were asked to develop plans for the next ten years. They were further asked to ignore the cost factor in this the initial phase of their plan, to open up their creative skills, uncovering their best dreams of what would be ideal. Their recommendations, delivered in the summer of 1968, were very thoughtful. The Study Councils appointed were: Agriculture, Biological Sciences, Economics and Business, Engineering, General Education, Home Economics, Humanities, Mathematics, Off-Campus Cooperative Extension, Off-Campus Research, Physical Sciences, Professional Education, Social Sciences, Student Life, Teacher Education, Veterinary Medicine and Pharmacy.

Contrary to many reports of this type, they were not ignored, shelved and forgotten. In fact, within a few years, many of their recommendations had been implemented. Their recommendations reflected recent developments in academic disciplines that had not been acted upon at WSU, as well as new recommendations for developments which they anticipated for the next ten years.

Summaries of the Study Council reports are in Appendix A. For those readers who have a desire for additional information about these important reports, I refer you to Professor George Frykman's book on the history of WSU, listed in the Bibliography. More information can be found at the WSU Library Archives. These reports provided the campus, faculty, students and staff an opportunity to speak independently about their dreams for the future. Also, I wanted to know if their major priorities were basically the same as mine. They were. Most recommended equally strong emphasis on undergraduate and graduate programs. Also, students expressed an important opinion about the poor communication between the students, administration and faculty, which I later offer as a factor in student unrest.

The appointment of the Study Councils was only one way of learning about WSU, and their reports convincingly portrayed their opinions of the present and their dreams of the future.

My desire to develop an understanding of the WSU culture also included sack lunch meetings with departments. I wanted to gain an understanding of what they thought was good as well as what they thought was not so good about their experiences at Washington State University. I wanted to know what their plans for the future were, and what the university could do to help them plan for and be optimistic about the future. I continued this program on a less frequent basis as long as I was there. In retrospect, I would have been better advised to have not reduced the frequency of these meetings.

I regarded it as equally important to maintain open communication with students as with faculty – in some instances, even more important. In fact, I became known as the "students' president," a designation that I agree with, and for good reason. They are the leaders of the next generation. I must add, however, that, as indicated earlier, my vision for WSU placed an equal emphasis on undergraduate and graduate programs and research.

I will elaborate on my relationship with students and faculties in subsequent chapters. For now, know that my initial efforts to become acquainted with students consisted primarily of my habit of showing up in the dormitory dining halls to join them in the lines to select lunch or dinner items and to sit with a group for conversations over the meals. I found these experiences interesting and even fun. Students opened up immediately since they seemed to sense that I respected them, and was very interested in hearing them talk about the good and the not so good about student life at WSU. Most of the time (except during student unrest in the late 1960s and early 1970s), I heard much more good than not so good. I also frequently accepted dinner invitations to sororities, fraternities, and those living in apartments off campus. On these occasions, it was an opportunity to engage the students in conversations about university policies with respect to academic and social issues. They were invariably frank about their opinions, which often proved helpful to me. I always enjoyed these discussions, even when we didn't agree with each other.

One of my goals in these contacts with students and faculty was to establish my accessibility. My long-suffering assistants, led by Gen DeVleming (the best assistant any university president anywhere ever had), quickly learned where I could be found, talking with students, faculty or both when I was scheduled to meet someone at the office or elsewhere. Gen did a fantastic job of getting faculty or students in to visit with me as soon as they called to make an appointment. University presidents can quickly become distant and impersonal figures if they are inaccessible to campus and off-campus constituents. I was determined that this would not happen to me. I regard this as a factor that resulted in my being included among the university presidents invited to the Wingspread Conference because of their successful management of the campus unrest period in American higher education.

Chapter Three

CAMPUS UNREST COMES EARLY

W hen I assumed the presidency at Washington State University, there were already campus demonstrations and protests in some states, particularly California. WSU students soon felt that it would be disgraceful if they sat quietly by and failed to become a part of the generation of students protesting such events as the Vietnam War, the reinstitution of the military draft, racism, and the failure of the curricula of universities and the older generation to address these problems.

The Colfax Scene

In mid-January, 1969, I was in Olympia, Washington attending the inaugural festivities for Governor Dan Evans. I was at the inaugural party in the governor's mansion, having a great time, when at 1:00am, I received a telephone call from one of Washington State's senators, Irv Newhouse, informing me of a fight at his son's AGR fraternity house in Pullman earlier that evening. The senator told me that a group of students had invaded the house and fought with some of the members. He further told me that one of the students who entered the house had a gun and fired it into the ceiling. Fortunately, no one was hit.

This conversation was followed by two hours on the phone with my assistant, Denny Morrison, in Pullman who, along with campus police, was investigating the incident, which had been provoked earlier in the day during an intramural basketball game. I did not sleep very well the rest of the night. The best measure of how things were managed, that night and subsequently, lies in the fact that Senator Newhouse and I are very good friends 34 years later. I am grateful to Art McCartan, Jack Clevenger and Denny Morrison for the excellent way they performed their duties.

This event caused a several-month furor on campus. The students, four or five as I remember, all African-Americans, who entered the fraternity house were tried in the Superior Court in Colfax and convicted of assault. When the deputy sheriff of Whitman County came to Pullman to pick up the students to take them to jail in Colfax, they were surrounded by dozens of other students, sympathizers and protesters, who followed them to Colfax, about ten miles away. When they arrived in Colfax, the protesters surrounded the students and blocked the efforts of the sheriff to put them in jail. A potentially dangerous scene developed when the protesters started shouting and throwing rocks at the jail. Fortunately, a faculty member from WSU, Jonnetta Cole, called me from the sheriff's office to discuss what should be done to reduce the tension, which was escalating by the minute. I could hear the shouting and threats increasing in volume.

I asked to speak with the sheriff, Mike Humphrey. The sheriff was very calm. We discussed several alternative actions, including further attempts to calm the crowd so that the students could be jailed. It became increasingly obvious that this was not possible without risking the lives of all involved. There were reports that angry vigilante groups were threatening to force action, which did not make the situation any easier. I suggested to Mike that he jail the entire group. His response was that he did not have room for all of them.

Darkness was descending on this normally quiet rural town. Someone in my office, Art McCartan, who was Dean of Men, I believe, suggested that all of the protesters and the students they were supporting be housed for the night in one of the churches in Colfax. Then, all of them would be taken to Spokane the next morning, where there was sufficient jail space. The sheriff bought this idea, as did the protesters. Thus, a creative solution was reached due to the calm, reasoned approach of Sheriff Humphrey, good staff work at WSU and the assistance of the WSU faculty member, Jonnetta Cole, advising the protesters. A potentially serious tragedy was avoided.

Alas, as is so often the case, not everyone agreed with the way it was handled. Our detractors wanted a more aggressive handling of these events. Some were particularly upset by the fact that WSU staff provided hamburgers, beverages and blankets for the group in the Colfax church. It is important to me that you know I approved of this humane gesture.

The hero of this episode is Sheriff Humphrey. If he had been an excitable person, or a law enforcement officer who was unable to respond to the complexities of a potentially explosive, dangerous situation like the one which descended on him from a college town, lives could have been lost. For these reasons, I praise Mike Humphrey, a splendid public servant. It was heartwarming to me to learn that the Black Students Union, realizing the quality of the man, sent him a dozen roses. Few things touched my heart in my eighteen years of service to WSU as deeply as the gift to Mike from this student group.

What principle, theory, idea or assumption about a university is apparent in the management or leadership exercised in what I will call the Colfax scene? It is not complex. The focal point of the university is the student, undergraduate and graduate. We have the responsibility of attending to their intellectual, social and personal development. The more I worked with students in the learning environment, the more I respected them, and the more I enjoyed them.

I dislike the term "customer" as applied to students, but we who lead and teach in colleges and universities are there for the intellectual and personal development of the students. We can do a better job in our leadership responsibilities in universities if we believe in the students' potential, and are willing to give them responsibilities. Admittedly, they sometimes disappoint us. However, making mistakes sometimes is as important (or more so) as successes in human development. The Colfax scene is not the only manifestation of my belief in the central role of the student in university organizations. As you will observe, that simple notion provided a basis or explanation for many decisions I made at Washington State University. Other assumptions will help explain why other decisions were made. And I confess, some issues came up so suddenly that it became necessary to rely entirely on instinct.

Sit-Ins, Strikes and Demonstrations

The Colfax events marked the beginning of organized student activism, or if you prefer, campus unrest at WSU. There were rumblings of one sort or another before that, but the campus was not dominated by protests and demonstrations until the events at Colfax. Many African-Americans and others on campus interpreted the convictions of assault by the Colfax judge as racist in nature, and initially proceeded to seek help from the university to address racism in the court system, as well as in the university itself. A series of demands, some of them labeled non-negotiable, were made on the University, designed to eliminate both individual and institutional racism.

This form of activity directed toward racism was a part of many colleges and universities in the United States and many foreign countries, for what I believe were mainly justifiable reasons. The killings at Kent State and Jackson State Universities and the incursion into Cambodia during the Vietnam War added a new cause and protest energy to the activity on many campuses (and in many cities), including the campuses in the State of Washington. I was attending a meeting in Washington, DC when the Cambodian incursion occurred. I received a phone call informing me that French Administration Building was occupied by several hundred students, and that they were waiting for me. The days of referring to the appropriate administrative associates were over. The students went directly to the president on most issues.

When I arrived on campus about four in the afternoon, there were several hundred sweaty, impatient students with a sprinkling of involved and curious onlookers to greet me. I invited the leaders to join me in what was at that time the Regents room to discuss their reasons for taking up residence in the French Administration Building. They informed me that they wanted (in the popular word of the day, "demanded") me to write to President Nixon, telling him that Washington State University opposed the incursion into Cambodia and the Vietnam War. I explained that I could not speak for the university as they requested, excuse me, demanded that I do, that to do so would improperly politicize the university and that neither they nor I could represent the university on this issue for the simple reason that university members have different opinions on issues such as these. In order to avoid total rejection of their demands, I did tell them that I would write to the President to tell him that *some* members of the WSU community opposed the incursion and the war, which I did. (I received a polite answer from the President, thanking me for writing.) The demonstrators quietly left the building.

The handling of the sit-in demonstrates two organizational principles, one of which was the basis for administrative action – my confidence in the essential goodness and reasonableness of students, even some of those who were yelling at me during the early stages of the sit-in. I knew many of them, including the ASWSU president, Carlton Lewis, with whom I had many discussions. My relationships with students gave me an understanding of their values, what they were like, and what they were thinking about. My background in developmental psychology was an asset. The decision to write to President Nixon was a way of assuring them that I understood their concerns. My explanation as to why I could not say in the letter what they wanted me to say — the representation that WSU, as a university, opposed the Vietnam War and the incursion into Cambodia — some of them understood, certainly enough of them to result in their leaving the building. The principle involved here was to communicate with the President of the United States in such a way as to avoid taking a stand that would politicize the university and misrepresent some individuals and groups. Failure to do this would violate a fundamental purpose of a university as a place where complex political and social issues can be debated. Enough of the students understood this, or they probably would not have left the building.

Some of the media hammered me and my associates for what appeared to be a total capitulation to the protesters. Incomplete or misleading stories of the meeting with the protesters, often including a photo of the meetings, appeared in newspapers around the state. Telephone calls and letters poured in, most of which were negative in word and tone. The regents were deluged with questions and found it necessary to meet in executive session without me to compare notes on public reactions to the sit-in in the French Administration Building. This was the first and only such meeting of the Regents without my attendance, except when they were evaluating my performance and deciding about any changes in salary or other conditions of employment. I did not understand this decision to have me left out, until Regent Frances Owen explained what happened. The regents felt that they needed an opportunity to let off steam that had been accumulating from the many questions and criticisms *they* received about what was going on at WSU. Yet another example of Frances' wisdom.

Many letters were received from people around the state. I believe we answered all but one, which was so offensive that I did not believe it deserved a response.

The campus was far from being quiet after the sit-in at French Administration Building. The protestors decided to organize a strike on classes, not the most creative decision they made during this era, since most colleges and universities had strikes. They weren't about to be left out of the strike culture of that era! Students gathered at the entrances of classroom buildings and attempted to persuade students to not attend classes. I do not remember any violence, but many students resented the effort to prevent class attendance. Some students attempted to disrupt the campus by participating in a march on Stadium Way, a main road surrounding the campus. One automobile was struck by an object of some description, one of the few instances of damage to property.

Another demonstration that accompanied that "joyful" spring was an attempt to disrupt the annual parade of the ROTC cadets. It was a well-known fact that the demonstration was to take place. We had a meeting of the ROTC officers and some student cadets to discuss how we were to manage the parade. The officers and students were in agreement that we should be as low key as possible, even to go so far as to ignore attempts to disrupt the parade, as long as the demonstrators did not assault any of the participants or onlookers. Only one of the officers and none of the students seemed to think we should be tougher on the demonstrators. They seemed to understand that aggressive treatment would only make heroes or martyrs out of the demonstrators.

The demonstrators infiltrated the columns of cadets, taunted them verbally and with gestures, but did not block their activity. I was seated with one regent and surrounded by veterans of past wars, who expressed their disapproval in no uncertain terms, especially when several protestors dumped body parts of animals they had gotten from one of the meat departments in Pullman. The parade ended and spectators disappeared after making it clear to me that they expected the demonstrators to be disciplined. The demonstrators weren't punished, and the student cadets agreed with the decision not to do so – another confirmation of my belief that protestors are usually attempting to make a point. In this case, it was their opposition to the war and racism, with which I was in complete agreement. What I don't agree with is infringing on the rights of others in the expression of one's opinions and values.

Regent Harold Romberg, who attended the parade, and I went to Spokane afterwards. Although he is a proud veteran of World War II, as am I, he agreed with the handling of the demonstration. This was a relief for me. It illustrates another important principle supported by much research in social psychology. People who witness an event such as the parade frequently will have different impressions of what they saw. Additionally, media representatives describing events such as the parade – from reports from other media – may have very different perceptions of what actually happened had they witnessed the events. I am confident that Mr. Romberg, an excellent regent, open-minded and able to see all sides of an issue, initially would have had a different reaction if he had developed an opinion from media reports.

The Racism Workshop

The cumulative effect of the Colfax incident, the occupation of the administration building, the strike and the demonstration at the ROTC parade, raised emotions on campus to a level bordering on hysteria. As indicated earlier, racism was the major target at the outset, joined by the Vietnam War. In retrospect, it is my opinion that the overarching issue was racism. Initially, it involved African-American students, the Black Student Union (BSU) and white students. Somewhat later, it grew to include the concerns of Hispanic students, faculty and Native Americans. Still later came womens issues. This last was precipitated, in part, by the passage of Title IX, in 1972s Higher Education Act of Congress. Later still, we had concerns expressed by those of Asian-American background, for the most part, residents of Spokane.

Something constructive had to be done to provide opportunities for discussions in a seminar or workshop format to lower the rapidly rising tensions on campus. The University Senate, at a meeting in late spring of 1970, recommended that we hold two days of classes on racism the following fall. I whole-heartedly approved the recommendation, and a group was identified to plan the program. It is very important to understand that two days of classes on the topic racism were to be held in the fall. Thus, the decision was an educational decision.

As the time approached for the workshop, opposition developed, mostly from off-campus. A state legislator from Spokane and a student requested through a court order, that the Superior Court in Colfax order the workshop cancelled. I was served an injunction notice from the sheriff of Whitman County that the workshop was not to be held. I then asked Special Assistant Attorney General Lloyd Peterson, on assignment at WSU, to appear before the State Supreme Court in Olympia to request a stay of the Superior Court order cancelling the workshop. At the time, Lloyd had a full facial beard, which he wisely shaved without being asked to do so. (In those days the beard was often associated with activist inclinations.)

When news of the injunction spread throughout the campus, there was a rally of students in the Student Union Building. I met with them to tell them that we were making every effort to have the injunction overturned. Some of the students asked why I did not simply refuse to obey the court order. That question provided me with an opportunity to explain two reasons. One was the important responsibility we all had to seek remedies only by all legal means possible. The other prompted me to remind them that I would be of no value to the university if I were sitting in the Colfax jail.

The appeal was made to the Supreme Court for relief on the basis of the university's authority to establish educational policy. Thankfully, the Supreme Court agreed. Just before the workshop began, an associate of our attorney handed me a note indicating that the Supreme Court granted our request of a stay of the Superior Court order to cancel the workshop. That announcement was followed by thunderous applause from the thousands of participants.

Professor Jim Short, Director of the Social and Economic Science Research Center, (SESRC), analyzed a random sample of workshop participants and found that the response to the workshop was strongly supportive. Significantly, the residents of Pullman in attendance, as well as members of the university community, strongly agreed that the workshop was beneficial to the community, in terms of reducing racial tensions. Jim was asked to report the results of the analysis by SESRC to the regents, who were quite surprised and encouraged, since most of the letters they had received were critical. This research demonstrates the importance of being at the scene when making judgements about events such as the workshop.

The workshop was attended by several thousand people, including students, faculty and residents of Pullman. It had an extraordinarily calming effect on the campus, providing an opportunity for the speakers and the large audience to express their feelings about racism. It was a good action by the University Senate, not only because it was the right action, but because it made the point that the power to establish educational policy in American higher education is vested in the educational institutions themselves, through the Board of Regents. It also demonstrated in a dramatic way that in a democracy, we institute change by working within the system, and contrary to the popular view of the times, the system can and did work.

The Opposition to ROTC

One of the targets of demonstrations on many campuses, including WSU, was the opposition to ROTC. I was criticized by some because of my appointment to the Board of Visitors of Air University in Montgomery, Alabama, the headquarters of the ROTC and other U. S. Air Force programs. I considered resigning from the Board, but not for long. My remaining on the Board was an important symbol of my support for the ROTC programs as an important element of our national defense system. (It is interesting to note that some universities who eliminated these programs during those turbulent years later reinstated them, or have made attempts to do so.)

It is my strong belief that our responses to the sit-in at the administration building, the strike on classes and the workshop on racism were in the best interest of the university. There was a desperate need for action that would have a calming effect on the campus. No one was killed or injured, as was the case at some other universities, and to my knowledge there was only minor property damage. (The south stands of the stadium were destroyed by fire, but investigators never found out who did it.)

In our judgment, there was nothing taking place that would have justified calling in the police, which could have resulted in injuries or even the death of students and others, as was the case at other universities. Nevertheless, understandably, the sit-in, the strike and the workshop on racism all within a three-month time period was too much for some on- and off-campus people to understand. I had learned during my three years in the State of Washington that most people here wanted to know *what* was going on and *why*, and instinctively seemed to want to have confidence in leaders of public institutions. In other words, most people in Washington State are blessed with compassion and good will. Furthermore, there was much that was going on that I did not fully understand at the time.

Letters

Thirty-five faculty members composed and signed a very timely letter to "Washington State University Alumni and the Parents of Our Students." The Regents received a copy of this letter. The letter helped allay concerns of Regents, alumni and parents, and helped pave the way for a successful speaking tour of the State for me, which I shall explain later. I give much credit to the colleagues who helped in this very significant way. This was an act of loyalty to WSU on the part if these colleagues, which turned out to be enormously helpful to me at a very difficult time.

To: Washington State Alumni and the Parents of Our Students

The strike at Washington State University has ended. Spring-semester classes are over. Commencement exercises have been held. Most of the students have left. It now seems an appropriate time for us as members of the WSU faculty to pass on some thoughts about recent events on the campus to those who are particularly interested in both the present and the future of the university.

Many of you have undoubtedly been disturbed by what you have heard and read. It is difficult for someone off campus to realize what is happening at the university. Rumor, gossip, and even slander can add to the concern of those who have an affection for and an allegiance to the institution. There are many questions that you could ask. What was the strike about? What are these unfamiliar organizations- the Black Student Union, MECHA, the Three Forks Peace Coalition, the Third World group? Why did President Glenn Terrell even talk with those who presented him with demands? Were classes cancelled and why? Why weren't the "ringleaders" expelled? Were off-campus agitators involved? How extensive was vandalism on the campus? What is institutional racism? Has the university fallen into the hands of drug-using, bomb-setting, spoiled brats? Have the faculty and administration abdicated their responsibilities when threatened with violence? These are important questions, and we hope that we may provide at least partial answers.

Any understanding of recent events at WSU must be related to the tensions existing in American society as a whole. This statement has been made many times, but it is too often forgotten. All citizens are concerned about Vietnam, poverty, pollution, violence, and discord. Students are not indifferent to the problems of the off campus world. Nor would we want them to be. Many students at Washington State are energetic, ambitious, young people, full of ideas and quick to condemn what they regard — rightly or wrongly — as failings on the part of their elders. Many of their cultural attitudes and their behavioral patterns are markedly different from those of thirty, twenty, or even ten years ago. They are inquisitive and interesting people. And they are definitely not children, to be ordered about or ignored or arbitrarily punished. Any parent who honestly looks at his relationship to his own children realizes that it takes a special effort to listen, to understand, and to persuade. And all these difficulties are complicated at a university with over 13,000 bustling, argumentative, at times even cantankerous young people who are determined, in large part, to think their own thoughts and to make their own decisions.

THE SIT-IN
What could be called the spring troubles at WSU began in early May. There had been scattered events preceding that date. A demonstration against some Pullman merchants had resulted in vandalism. Arrests had been made, and cases growing out of the episode are now pending in court. On April 4, a fire — the result of arson — virtually destroyed the 10,000-seat south stands on Rogers Field. There had also been several peace demonstrations, an environmental teach-in, and other activities that indicated some unrest on campus.

On May 5, following the announcement by President Nixon that American troops were being sent into Cambodia and the deaths of four students at Kent State University in Ohio, approximately 700 people occupied the French Administration Building. There was no violence, but the demonstrators demanded that the university administration send a telegram to President Nixon urging immediate withdrawal of troops from Cambodia, censuring deaths on other university campuses, and issuing a statement demanding that National Guardsmen be withdrawn from all universities in the country.

President Terrell was not on campus when the occupation of the building began. He returned later that day and entered into discussions with those making the demands. After consultation with students, faculty, and administrative advisers, he sent a telegram to President Nixon. The telegram read: "The recent events on the campus of Kent State University and the

extension of the war in Cambodia have created
outrage and dismay on the part of a substantial segment of the campus at Washington State
University. You have observed similar reactions across the nation. Many on our campus
deplore the decision to send troops into Cambodia and the tragic deaths Monday of the four
students at Kent State." President Terrell also
announced that on May 7 the university would
hold a teach-in on Cambodia in place of the
regular class schedule. After this announcement, those occupying the building departed.

At this time, as later, there were complaints
— both on and off campus — about President
Terrell's actions. It is probably true that
anything he would have done would have offended many people. One fact, however, must be
accepted. Whatever anyone's personal opinion
about the movement of troops into Cambodia and
the events at Kent State, there is no question
but that these occurrences sent a shock wave
through American campuses. Student tempers were
aroused, and feelings ran high.

President Terrell was aware of this situation
and of the implications of his actions. When
he sent the telegram, he stressed that "I cannot speak for the entire university." He emphasized that the telegram would indicate only
that a sizable number of students at WSU de-
plored the move into Cambodia and the Kent
State incident. "I reached these decisions believing unequivocally that they were wise decisions. I am not defensive about them nor do
I make any apologies for either of them." Of
the telegram to President Nixon, he said: "I
did agree to write and did write to indicate
that many on campus were angered over this
decision. This is a statement of fact."

Concerning the decision to use a day for a
teach-in on Cambodia, he stated: "I made this

decision free of any threat of violence by the assembled students if this action were not taken. Rather, I made it because I was convinced as I talked with faculty, students, and administrative advisors that this would be a constructive way for the WSU community to exchange views about the pros and cons of the war and a far better way of letting off steam than through the destructive actions which have occurred on so many campuses. I have urged those organizing the teach-in to achieve a balance of those opposing and supporting the extension of the war in Cambodia."

And he also pointed out that he anticipated criticism. "Some will say if a university agrees to these demands it will be pressured to agree to others also. I do not subscribe to that position. In the past we have rejected requests that we regard to be not in the best interests of the university. We shall continue to do so."

THE STRIKE

Off-campus events - the killing of students at Jackson State and the deaths in Augusta, Georgia - were at least partially responsible for the campus crisis occurring in the middle of the month. On May 18, representatives of several student groups (the most prominent of which were the Black Student Union and MECHA- the Chicano students movement) addressed themselves to so-called Third World problems and presented eleven demands to President Terrell. Those announcing the demands stated that "the time has come to take meaningful and effective steps to eliminate racism from our institution." The demands were prompted by the belief of the Black and Chicano students (and, as it turned out, by large numbers of other students) that personal acts of racism and certain built-in institutional practices were intolerable and that the university should end such acts and such practices. Most of you are probably familiar with the eleven demands. Briefly, they were as follows, and demanded that the university:

1. Immediately disarm all campus police and the ROTC and disavow the use of violence (for instance, National Guard, Highway Patrol, etc.) on campus to disrupt demonstrations.

2. Eliminate all plainclothes and undercover agents (including FBI), cease the compilation of faculty and student dossiers for the purpose of political blackmail, and prohibit university personnel from engaging in undercover work or gathering evidence for punitive actions.

3. Establish a Review Board, consisting of Third World people, elected by campus Third World organizations, to investigate all law-enforcement actions involving Third World people and political cases both on and off campus.

4. Use its legal and financial resources as well as its influence to present a constitutional challenge before the courts to determine the right of Third World defendants to be tried in such a manner and in such a place as will ensure a fair trial and that they be tried and judged by their peers from the Third World.

5. Immediately abolish the university disciplinary board.

6. Establish a Third World board elected by campus Third World organizations with which the publications board will be required to work in fighting racism on campus.

7. Conduct a ten-day racism workshop which shall be mandatory for all faculty, staff, and administration members, to be given at the

beginning of the fall semester, and conducted by faculty and students in programs
in American minorities studies.

8. Immediately hire three Third World admissions officers whose sole responsibility
will be to accelerate recruiting of Third
World students.

9. Achieve a racial balance of Third World
people proportional to their numbers in the
U.S. population among undergraduate and
graduate students, and on the faculty, staff,
and administration and the Board of Regents, within three years.

10. Not allow any repetition of the loss of key
faculty members which now threatens the vi-
ability of the Black Studies Program.

11. Immediately remove all non-union grapes from
campus.

On May 22, by means of an open letter to members of the university community, President
Terrell responded to the eleven demands. Although he rejected all eleven demands, he did
so in a reasonable and objective manner which
some may feel was too conciliatory. He pointed
out that so long as the campus police func-
tioned as part of campus security, it was foolish to disarm them and that ROTC rifles did not
have any firing mechanisms. He stated his confidence that the campus could solve its problems without calling on outside law-enforcement
agencies for help, and that he would rely upon
such outside forces only if absolutely necessary. He pointed out that the university does
not maintain dossiers on faculty and students
for any political purpose, and that city and
county police have the legal right to be on
campus when engaged in legitimate law-enforcement activities. He refused to establish spe-

cial tribunals for special groups of people and pointed out that the university has various mechanisms at hand for dealing with the problems of minority students. He stated that the university does not have the authority to conduct litigation on behalf of individuals and that representation of individuals charged with offenses in courts is outside the scope of the university's mission of education and learning.

President Terrell said that abolition of the disciplinary board would mean that the university had no responsibility for the conduct of its students. "We are not disposed to take the position that the university should give up its responsibility to make independent judgments about the behavior of faculty, staff, and students." He stated that he was asking the Human Relations Committee to address itself to questions associated with equality of life for all minorities in all facets of university life, including student publications. He said that there are already in existence various workshops on racism on campus and that plans for additional similar activities are under way. But he pointed out that he could only urge, not force, faculty, students, and staff to attend. The university, he said, is engaged in special efforts to recruit minority students and will continue to do so, although there were various factors that made it impossible to assume that the university could achieve the balance demanded. He also explained the resignations of several faculty members involved in the Black Studies Program and stressed the university's commitment to the Program.

President Terrell closed his letter: "We must redouble our efforts to find solutions to problems of racial discrimination. We must use reason, dialogue, and appropriate action. Racial violence and racial inequities will not be solved by countering threats of violence. The university is not a place where solutions should be sought in an atmosphere of confrontation and threats. Our resources can be much better spent in seeking solutions through the application of intelligent search, dialogue, and peaceful action among members of a committed community."

On the evening of May 22, there was a rally of over 1,000 students. Here a vote was taken to strike the university until the Third World students were satisfied that their grievances had been redressed. The call for the strike said that this action "does not necessarily mean that all the demands would be met in toto; that is for the Third World groups to decide." In other words, the strike was in support of the Third World students, and the course the strike would take would be influenced by the success the university and the Third World students achieved in reconciling their differences.

Who were the strikers? As always, it is difficult to give exact descriptions of members of a group action or to state with certainty the motivations of everyone who took part. Some participating students (undoubtedly a small minority) were those prepared to take advantage of any opportunity to slam the "establishment." Some students took part just for the hell of it. But the great majority of the strikers were sincerely concerned about the issue of racism. The various strike meetings attracted up to 3,000 people (more than gather at the usual football rally), and almost everyone who had the opportunity to attend any of these gatherings was impressed by the seriousness, the dedication, and the feelings of the assembled students.

Support for the strike was widespread. Students and faculty in departments such as plant pathology, psychology, economics, mathematics, chemistry, fine arts, and others went on record as supporting the general thrust of the strike. Many fraternities, sororities, and residence halls voted overwhelmingly to announce their opposition to racism. Even among many students who did not participate there was a great measure of sympathy for the announced aims of the strike action.

There was opposition to the strike. Some students were opposed to anything that might interfere with their classroom activities. On May 26 a group of students and faculty organized themselves as a University Committee for Rationality. This organization issued the following statement: "We strongly urge the university and individual members of the university community to work for the improvement of race relationships, but we disapprove of the strike as a method, and categorically oppose the participation of university employees in the strike." In addition, there were many off-campus people who indicated their belief that the strike should not be tolerated and that the university should act to end the strike.

The university administration adopted the policy of keeping the university open and of making itself available at all times for discussions. On May 25, the Vice President-Academic issued a statement to the faculty. "Classes will be held during the week of May 25-30 as scheduled. It is expected that all members of the faculty and all teaching assistants will discharge their instructional duties in accordance with their responsibilities to the university and to those students who wish to continue their studies without interruption. The university is firmly committed to increasing the strength and scope of its Minority Studies Program and to attacking racial discrimination in all its forms. A cessation of the instructional process cannot contribute to the attainment of these goals."

RESOLUTION OF THE STRIKE

On June 1, President Terrell announced that the university administration, the Black Student Union, MECHA, and the chairmen of the Faculty Executive and Educational Policies committees had arrived at an agreement, largely a restatement of what he had suggested the university was prepared to do. The following decisions had been accepted by all. A special assistant to the president for minority affairs would be appointed. The new assistant would be responsible for investigating instances of racial discrimination on campus and for making recommendations regarding steps to be taken to improve the total campus environment for minority group members.

Six students-two Blacks, two Chicanos, and two American Indians-will be appointed by the new special assistant following recommendation by the BSU, MECHA, and the American Indian Student Association. This council will work closely with the special assistant to the president and with various student, faculty, staff, and outside agencies.

A number of racism workshops and other programs have been planned for the campus this fall. The university also pledged itself, so far as legally possible, to cooperate with the State Board Against Discrimination in its efforts to combat racial discrimination in all segments of society. Two Chicano students have been employed one-quarter time in the Admissions Office next year to assist in the recruiting of Chicano students. The Director of Admissions will employ two Black students and two American Indian students - also one-quarter time - to assist in recruiting students from these groups.

That evening the final strike rally was held. Representatives of the Black Student Union and MECHA announced that they had arrived at meaningful and satisfactory conclusions with the university and that, therefore, the reasons for the strike no longer existed. The strike was then declared at an end.

COMMENTS ON THE STRIKE

It is difficult to make generalizations about any event, and interpretations will differ, depending upon the observer and his point of view. Perhaps the best approach would be to attempt some answers to questions that have been asked about recent occurrences at the university.

How much violence occurred?

There were some instances of violence during the strike. The windshield of a passing vehicle was shattered by a piece of wood thrown by a non-student. Legal action in this matter is now proceeding. There were several bomb scares, and one fire bomb was discovered. The Student Bookstore had three windows smashed, and an early-morning fire on May 29 - unquestionably an arson attempt - damaged about forty seats on the north (sic) side of Rogers Field.

Yet one of the significant aspects of the strike was its consistent non-violent character. There were no dangerous confrontations with campus police (indeed, on one occasion the campus police chief was applauded when he addressed the strikers). There was no rock-throwing. There was no flag-burning. There was a noticeable absence of the empty-headed exhibitionism that has plagued so many campuses. In the face of persistent rumors (armed forces had set up camp outside Pullman, professional revolutionaries were being imported, bounties were being placed on the heads of those regarded as strike leaders, etc.), events never got out of control. At strike meetings, every suggestion that some act of violence be undertaken was immediately rejected. Although picket lines were thrown up around classroom buildings, force was not used to keep students from attending classes, and we found no evidence of physical assault on anyone during the strike.

On May 23, President Terrell and Pullman City Supervisor Larry Larse issued a statement. "Inflammatory rumors Thursday and Friday were rampant both in downtown Pullman and on the WSU campus. The students of WSU and the residents of the Pullman area have been remarkably calm in the face of these rumors, and for this they have our praise and respect." It might be worthwhile to quote from a letter to President Terrell written by a student on May 27. "All the students have demonstrated that they can voice their opinions in a sane fashion and without violence, destruction, or killing. We have also demonstrated to the people of this community that we can, and will continue to, talk openly and freely and we encourage them to do the same. We are proud to be able to say that our university has remained nonviolent - and has kept its door open at a time when many others have been forced to close and send everyone home."

Was the strike over serious matters?
The strike was not a childish prank. It was a serious activity by students concerned with a serious problem. Put bluntly, it was an expression of student anxiety over the problem of individual and institutional racism. It is somewhat difficult for many older people to realize how concerned many students are about racial discrimination and about the subtle and not-so-subtle ways members of minority groups are continually reminded of what many of their fellow-citizens consciously or unconsciously think of them. We all know that Blacks, Mexican-Americans, and American Indians live in an

environment consisting of the sly remark, the patronizing gesture, the only slightly disguised affront. In housing arrangements, in social activities, in their contacts with people, minority students are confronted with frustrating and insulting evidence of the disregard in which they are held.

The official position of Washington State University on the question of racism is strong and steady. In an open letter to students on May 27, President Terrell stated that he "opposes racism in any form" and that the WSU administration "is dedicated to the struggle to eliminate it." He said that his opposition to racism "is the social problem about which I have the strongest personal commitment."

Yet there is evidence that personal and institutional racism does exist at this university, as it does in most areas of our society. Minority students are regarded with hostility by some employees of the university, and certain established institutional patterns do discriminate against such students. Those striking - and large numbers of those who did not strike - were determined that WSU should do everything possible to eliminate any trace of racism on campus. One indication of student attitude here was the response to the possibility that black students might withdraw from WSU. Many non-striking students were shocked and appalled at the idea of WSU becoming a lily-white institution. In the second half of the twentieth century such a university would be a monstrosity and would be so divorced from what is going on in American life as to violate all the principles to which WSU has pledged itself for eighty years.

Why was force not used to subdue those who were disrupting the routine of the campus? Large numbers of people are angry about campus disorders and believe that the university should "crack down" on malcontents. We can understand this anger, and certainly a university should seek outside help if life or property is being threatened. But this was not the case at WSU. We feel that troops and police should be brought to the campus only when every other method of resolving the crisis has failed. It is easy to speak of calling in the troops. But the history of campus disorders indicates that the introduction of troops or police onto a campus immediately leads to intensified conflict. In Ohio, California, Iowa, Wisconsin, Maryland, and other states off-campus police and military personnel have moved onto campuses. The results of such intervention have usually been disastrous to the educational programs of such universities, and this spring over 200 of them were in various states of closure. In most cases when outside force is used on campus, the chief victims have been students who were not originally involved in the disruption and who wished only to continue with their studies. The result of armed intervention is highly unpredictable, and we should remember that the great majority of those students killed this spring have been uncommitted bystanders.

WSU's principal responsibility is to provide educational opportunities for its students. It is not primarily a disciplinary organization, designed to expel students, to break strikes, or to use brutal force against any members of the university community. We think there are better ways to settle campus disputes, and the history of the recent strike indicates that WSU may be uniquely prepared to keep such disputes from tearing the school to pieces.

Can President Terrell handle the situation at WSU?

The attacks upon President Terrell have distressed us. Many of these adverse comments are based upon false information and misunderstanding. As we look back over the events of May, it is obvious that President Terrell did not lose control of the situation. He was dedicated to keeping the university open, to avoiding the use of force, and to carrying on discussions with striking students. He maintained his balance in spite of insults that came from some students and from many interested off-campus people. He did not allow himself to become provoked. He listened to students without being patronizing, and he seemed to be searching at all times for a solution that would be honest, fair, and practical. He was not "faked" into verbal explosions or into abandoning his belief that the university must solve its own difficulties.

President Terrell has been accused of failing to show "guts." This complaint is unfair and untrue. It is easy to bluster about and to threaten and to make statements designed for exciting newspaper reading. It is easy to pose as a military commander and to rush in with flailing arms and angry words. Patience in the midst of threatened disorder is not weakness; rather, it is the undertaking of rash action that usually indicates that the situation is out of hand and that the man in charge doesn't know what he is doing.

One final fact should be mentioned. In its final meeting of the year the Resident Instructional Staff by a majority vote adopted special grading procedures for this semester only. These procedures recognized that the stress of the preceding two weeks might unjustly penalize our students.

Our Appeal

The loyalty of alumni to WSU is well known. The university needs the support of alumni and parents. We are asking you to maintain your interest in the institution. Of course, there are many things about WSU that may irritate you, and certainly we on campus make mistakes. But it is easy to support a university when the weather is fair and there are no problems. Support is more meaningful when we face difficulties. There is a traditional American phrase that sums up our situation: "When the going gets tough, the tough get going." That is really what we are asking. For support from tough people — tough-minded individuals who are not shaken by rumors or petty dissatisfactions. We are not asking for unexamined approval. What we need is steady, critical determination to stick with the university and with us through some troublesome times.

We have dedicated ourselves to Washington State University, and most of us intend to spend a significant part of our adult lives here. We are not giving up on the university. And why should we? WSU is not, as some have suggested, on the verge of disaster. Our undergraduate program next fall will be the most exciting and varied in the school's history. Our research efforts in many areas continue to contribute increasingly to the health and prosperity of the state. We are enrolling an ever-larger number of students from all parts of Washington who expect WSU to provide quality education and the opportunity to prepare themselves for satisfying professional careers.

This then is our case. We thank you for any consideration the matters we have discussed here may receive. We would be happy to receive your comments on these subjects, to have you visit the campus, or to send a representative of the faculty to meet with any small or large group desiring to speak further about our mutual concerns.

- Edward M. Bennett, Associate Professor of History
- V.N. Bhatia, Professor of Pharmacy
- Charles E. Blackburn, Associate Professor of English
- Donald W. Bushaw, Professor of Mathematics
- Alfred B. Butler, Professor of Physics and Physical Sciences
- Victor L. Dauer, Professor of Physical Education for Men
- Richard D. Daugherty, Professor of Anthropology
- John R. Elwood, Professor of English
- Mary Lou Enberg, Associate Professor of Physical Education for Women
- Remo Fausti, Professor of Speech
- Mary Gallwey, Associate Professor of Child and Family Studies
- Henry Grosshans, University Editor and Lecturer in History
- Elizabeth R. Hall, Professor of Bacteriology and Public Health
- Richard D. Harbour, Associate Professor of Electrical Engineering
- William H. Hayes, Associate Professor of Philosophy
- Adolph Hecht, Professor of Botany and Genetics
- Eldon Hendriksen, Professor of Business Administration
- William Iulo, Professor of Economics
- Leo Jensen, Professor of Poultry Science
- Paul A. Klavano, Professor of Veterinary Physiology and Pharmacology
- John D. Lillywhite, Professor of Sociology
- Charles F. Martin, Professor of Pharmaceutical Chemistry
- Gordon E. McCloskey, Professor of Education
- Charles W. McNeil, Professor of Zoology and General Biology

- Raymond Muse, Professor of History

- Robert A. Nilan, Professor of Genetics and Agronomy

- Antoinette A. Poulsen, Associate Professor of Foreign Languages

- Hugh A. Rundell, Associate Professor of Communications

- Gordon Rutherford, Associate Professor of Education

- Frances Sadoff, Associate Professor of Office Administration

- David M. Scott, Professor of Architecture

- Carl M. Stevens, Professor of Biochemistry

- James J. Sweeney, Head Football Coach

- James E. Whipple, Professor of Psychology

Note: This is not an official statement of the Washington State University administration, nor is it an "official" statement of the university faculty. It is merely an attempt by those whose names appear above to inform you.

I received many notes and phone calls from faculty members, in addition to the one printed above. Some were supportive and some were not. I include below the most negative letter I received, apparently from six faculty members who did not identify themselves.

The WSU Campus
June 1, 1970

Dr. Glenn Terrell, President
Washington State University
613 Campus Ave.
Pullman, Washington 99163

Dear Sir,

We are six members of the WSU Faculty who wish to express our great concern for the future of this University. We are not from a single area or department. In fact, we represent four different Colleges. Neither are we black, nor do we wear beards, or do we rabble-rouse. Some of us are closer to you than you might suspect. We aren't signing our names because we now know how you operate, and it might not go well for certain of us in the future — that is while you are still on campus.

Dr. Terrell, you have betrayed the faculty and the students of this University. And in so doing, you have lost the faith and the respect and the trust of the largest majority of us. Not only here at the University, but throughout the State. You have also lost the faith and respect and the trust of the community of Pullman and of the members of the WSU Alumni Association as well. We no longer believe in you. And we can no longer look to you with respect and loyalty. You can no longer be an effective leader of the employees of this University. You may be our shortest term President.

It might be very difficult for you to believe, but you are actually the laughing stock in many conversations both on and off the campus at this time. (But, it is really too serious to be a laughing matter.) It is really rather pitiful, and we are very sorry to see and hear it — but we are certain that you will probably be the last to know.

We have heard it said that you actually believe that you are doing a good job. How unfortunate that you, a psychologist, can be so blind. Or don't you really care? You also think you are doing a good job with and for the students. But, Sir, even Carlton Lewis, the ASWSU President-elect openly stated — right on the front page of the Evergreen — that what you say, and what you mean are two different things. Dr. Terrell, the students don't trust you either.

Last Thursday at the faculty meeting, even when

you made a particularly favorable point, did you notice that not more than one third of the Faculty stood up for you? The rest of us cannot stand up for you, or with you in the future. We have been hopeful for three years, but now we know that you have failed us. You and your clenched fist as a sign of victory — Bah! And we actually do favor the minor study programs — that is not the point, or the issue.

On May 22 when you defied the faculty and students by capitulating to that small howling mob of radicals in the French Administration Building, you truly alienated no less than 90 percent of the University personnel. Never have we seen so many irate and disgusted people on this campus before. You lost more of us right there. That was a turning point. It was a time to stand up and be counted. You you (sic), Sir, did not have the guts to do what needed to be done. You showed us what you are made of, and we don't buy it.

We are now convinced that the only reason that you have said "no" to most of the eleven de- mands in the current crisis is because Mr. Harold Romberg said "no" first. Statewide, as well as on the campus, most everyone believes that Mr. Romberg said "no" first because even he feared that you alone would say "yes."

Most of the faculty members and the students know that you are lying when you say that everything possible was done to keep Mr. & Mrs. Robert Cole at WSU. We know the truth of the matter is that the entire Department of Economics has been trying everything possible to get rid of Cole for a long time. (Inciden- tally, none of us who are writing this letter is in the Department of Economics — so please don't jump on them.) By the way, when it was finally announced that the Coles were actually leaving, it was the best news we have had here on this campus for a long time.

The final blow to your trust with the faculty came when you publicly announced that you had offered to match the Coles' salary offer from the Eastern School in order to get them to remain at WSU. Even those faculty members who hadn't already been alienated were infurated (sic) by that disclosure. Sir, it has been the policy of this institution for all of it's (sic) long history, and furthermore, it is quoted in the Faculty Manual that, "As a policy, change in rank or salary will not be made to meet the competitive offer of another institution". Just what kind of administrative integrity is that? And, besides, it (the offer) was made to undesirable radicals who most of us are happy to see leave. Just what could you expect the majority of the faculty members to think? Or dn't (sic) you really care?

Mr. Terrell, you are going to be a short term President. Even if you do not resign, you will never regain the confidence of the WSU Faculty Members. We simply can not be loyal to a President with such poor administrative judgment. And we six know that this is the feeling of most of the Staff, the Faculty, and large numbers of Students at Washington State University.

These are strong, stern words, but Mr. Terrell, you had better believe that they are true, and are written for the future betterment of this University.

A Group of WSU Faculty Members

Copies to:
Members of the Board of Regents
Dr. Wallis Beasley

After the campus calmed down somewhat (actually, on a college campus there is a constant bubbling of some sort), I scheduled a speaking tour of the state, meeting with community leaders, civic clubs, editorial boards of newspapers, alumni, and state officials. It was heart-warming to be given standing ovations after speaking to many groups. Each meeting included an opportunity to ask questions. In part, they were telling me that they appreciated the fact that I wanted to meet with them, that I had given them an opportunity to ask questions, and that I had expressed an understanding of why they were curious, angry or upset. Editorial Board members of the state's newspapers also, for the most part, understood. I say this because citizens throughout the state, including Editorial Board members, alumni, state officials, including the governors and legislators supported me throughout the rest of my tenure, with one minor exception that I shall explain later.

I especially appreciate the strong support of then-Governor Dan Evans, whose terms of office included the campus activism period. He was a tower of strength, steady, insightful, and the students loved him. He had a way with them, which enabled him to establish immediate rapport. During his frequent visits to the WSU campus, he generally met with student groups, sometimes angry groups, and never failed to win them over. In my opinion, it was his respect for them that came through. Governor Evans also delivered timely radio and television messages that had a calming effect on citizens disturbed over campus activism. Our problems would have been more serious without his excellent leadership.

Race Issues

Although in the earlier days, beginning with the Alpha Gamma Rho fraternity and Colfax incidents in the winter and spring of 1969, student activism was directed mainly toward discrimination of African-Americans on and off campus. As mentioned earlier, there was also early participation by MECHA (a Hispanic group) and Native American students. The leaders of these groups were Ernie Thomas and Ron Taplin, African-Americans; Ky Tecumseh and Matt Wanchena, Native Americans; and Tomas Ybarra, Margarita Mendoza de Sugiyama and Zeneido Comacho for MECHA. These three groups generally worked cooperatively.

However, it was my impression that the Native American group participated in discussions and actions on issues which they thought served the interests of their group.

All of the student leaders listed in the previous paragraph were very talented, as indicated by their current positions: Ky Tecumseh is working for the U.S. Department of Defense in Albuquerque, New Mexico; Ernie Thomas is the President of Tarrant County Community College South in Ft. Worth, Texas; Margarita Mendoza de Sugiyama directs consumer services for the Attorney General's office in Seattle, Washington; Matt Wanchena is on the Woodinville, Washington city staff; Zeneido Comacho is on the faculty at Baylor University College of Medicine; Tomas Ybarra is Dean of Student Affairs at Bellevue Community College in Bellevue, Washington; Ron Taplin is Associate Dean of Student Affairs at Bellevue Community College in Bellevue, Washington; and Ernie Thomas was the Vice President for Student Affairs at Evergreen State College prior to accepting the presidency of Tarrant County Community College South.

I am very proud of these leaders, and their accomplishments. I recognized all of them as having outstanding leadership ability as undergraduate students. I mention these former students because those who did not know them and their roles during the student protest movement at WSU, may remember only the unrest they helped generate. Those of us who knew them well saw their potential for good leadership, which is always in short supply. They could not conceal the good side of themselves from me. In fact, I felt a kinship to all of them even when they were yelling at me. After all, they were trying to help rid the world of war and racism, something all of us should be working on. As I am confident they understood, we had our differences only as to how we should work to bring these changes about.

I have an amusing true story to relate about Ernie Thomas. When he was at Evergreen State College, responsible for student affairs, he had a demonstration by students in his office, protesting against a policy issue. One day when I was on the way to my office at The Pacific Institute, I heard over the radio that the students were focusing their displeasure on Ernie and his office. I have to admit that I found it very difficult to wait until I reached my office to call Ernie to needle him a bit. When I called him, he said the students were yelling at him the way they did at me 25 years ago at WSU.

MECHA focused on the racist treatment of farm workers in Washington and California. They reminded us that the university was purchasing grapes and lettuce harvested by a union that was unfair in its treatment of farm workers. One of their goals was to persuade the university to purchase grapes and lettuce harvested only by Chavez's United Farm Workers Union.

Several incidents occurred in downtown Pullman that further antagonized and even frightened local citizens. A few individuals expressed their anger by throwing grapes on the floors of local grocery stores and crushing them with their feet, I presume believing they were harvested by someone other than the United Farm Workers union.

As mentioned above, the Hispanic group also insisted that the university serve only lettuce harvested by the United Farm Workers Union. We decided to let the students in the dormitories decide the issue by vote. For food service in the student union, a public eating place, we gave the customer the choice.

Gender Issues

In 1972, Title IX of the Higher Education Act was passed by Congress requiring equality of opportunity for women and men in athletics. The congressional act was totally fair. It did, however, present a serious financial problem, particularly for WSU and other universities with limited income from intercollegiate athletics. WSU was already receiving several hundred thousand dollars for athletics from the state's general fund, which led to another problem with some faculty members. Football was the only sport that produced income. Initially, more funds were awarded to women's sports, but not enough to satisfy the Title IX requirements.

Some women students and faculty members brought a lawsuit against the university and me for failing to meet the requirements of Title IX. In the State of Washington, the Attorney General advises and defends the universities. I just needed to be sure that I was discharging my duties as president in a prudent manner. What did bother me were the same things that bothered me about the war and racism. War is a horribly primitive way to settle differences, and racism is horribly unfair. Discrimination because of gender and age fall in the same category. I now notice the discrimination against the elderly on occasion. Interestingly, I found that, generally, the public perception of me when I was in my 70s was that I was an "old" man. But on my 80th birthday, two years ago, the perception changed from "old" to "wise." Usually, I find humor when someone, say a clerk in a store, addresses all comments and questions to my wife, who is 14 years younger than I am, as if I'm too old to understand. But, occasionally, my sense of humor fails me, and I feel at least a slight sting.

Back to Title IX. Our problem was that we did not have the financial resources to meet the challenge of immediately equalizing opportunity for women while not making drastic cuts in long-established men's programs. However, reductions were made in men's sports, For example, we eliminated competitive programs in swimming and wrestling, and reduced the funding in most non-revenue producing programs. But the gradual elimination of unequal opportunity, for reasons of gender and race, did not satisfy the women and the ethnic minority groups, just as the gradual elimination of age discrimination is not enough for me, now that I am a "wise" man. It is my understanding that Title IX requirements are now being met.

Were the decisions made during the campus activism based on organizational theory? Yes and no. I'll have to explain that. To have agreed to many of the eleven demands (mentioned in the faculty letter) would have violated an ancient concept of the university as a community of scholars committed to the search for truths. This concept is a protection of the people who created the university. Without this protection, many of the discoveries beneficial to society would never have happened. Further, adherence to this concept makes it essential that the university be a place where opinions are expressed freely, and where members of the university community may pursue research interests and publish results free of restrictions within or outside the university.

As mentioned earlier, I was issued demands that I speak for the university on controversial issues like the war in Vietnam. To have agreed to them would have been misleading, for the simple reason that many in the university did not agree with what was being asked. More important, to have acceded to the demand would have thrust the university into involvement in a politically controversial issue. I explained to them that the role of the university was to provide a place where controversial issues like the war could be debated, and that the proclamation by the president would have a tendency to stifle debate.

The more militant protesters cared nothing about university organizational theory. In fact, the more I offered this as a reason I could not grant some of their demands, the more contentious the militant demonstrators became. How could I connect with them? By the simple acknowledgment that I agreed with them, personally, on their opposition to wars of any kind except in self-defense, and specifically, the Vietnam War; and on the despicable evils of unequal opportunity on the basis of race, gender and age. This satisfied some of the demonstrators.

Good things happened as a result of campus activism:
1. There was a highly desirable increase in the awareness of unequal opportunity in the world, and of the responsibility of all of us to oppose it in any form. WSU took steps to eliminate it on campus.
2. Programs in African-American, Native-American and Hispanic-American studies were established.
3. More aggressive recruiting of multicultural faculty, students and staff was instituted. Table One on page 59 contains the total numbers and percentages of the student body of Asian-American, African-American, Native-American and Hispanic heritage from 1968 to 2001. As can be seen in Table One, the total ethnic enrollment increased from 310 (2.6% of the total

enrollment in 1968) to 2,356 (13.1% of the total enrollment) in 2001. Head count increases in Asian-American, African-American, Native-American and Hispanics were 171 to 955, 84 to 542, 23 to 267 and 32 to 592 respectively. The data include enrollments for all campuses. No statistics were collected for 1969 and 1971. Also, data for 1972 were collected from the optional data cards distributed in registration packets, and in 1973 the data were collected from the optional data cards in admission applications. Since 1975, the data have been collected from admission applications. I thank Steve Nakata of Multicultural Student Services for this information.

4. Several African-American men and women have been appointed to major administrative positions, including Dr. John Slaughter and Dr. Al Yates, both as Vice-President and Provost; four women, Dr. Lois DeFleur and more recently, Dr. Barbara Couture have been appointed Dean of the College of Liberal Arts, while Dr. Judy Mitchell is now Dean of the College of Education. Dr. DeFleur is now the very successful President of Binghamton University, State University of New York. Dr. Virginia Steele is Director of Libraries. George Raveling was head coach of Men's Basketball for eleven years, and Paul Graham also Men's Basketball head coach.

5. An African-American man, Dr. Les Purce, who worked with student affairs from 1970-72, and later in the 1990s in university relations, is now the President of Evergreen State College in Olympia, Washington. Dr. Purce received his Ph.D. degree from Idaho State University. I met him earlier when I was visiting Idaho State. He was very effective during the student activism era and later in university relations.

6. Professor Talmadge Anderson established and edited the Journal of Black Studies.

7. The establishment of the program, Multicultural Student Services, in more recent years.

8. The establishment of the University Senate with student membership.

9. The establishment of Ethnic Minorities Studies.

Table One
Ethnic Enrollment: Fall Semester 1968-2001

Year	Asian-American Head Count	%	African-American Head Count	%	Native-American Head Count	%	Hispanic Head Count	%	Total Head Count	%
1968	171	1.4	84	0.7	23	0.2	32	0.3	310	2.6
1969										
1970	203	1.4	132	0.9	33	0.2	38	0.3	406	2.8
1971										
1972	195	1.3	164	1.1	107	0.7	91	0.6	557	3.8
1973	201	1.4	248	1.7	109	0.7	94	0.6	652	4.4
1974	221	1.4	302	1.9	128	0.8	113	0.7	764	4.9
1975	226	1.4	314	1.9	111	0.7	144	0.9	795	4.9
1976	218	1.3	295	1.8	120	0.7	165	1.0	798	4.8
1977	244	1.5	256	1.5	132	0.8	157	.09	789	4.7
1978	272	1.6	279	1.7	133	0.8	168	1.0	852	5.1
1979	291	1.7	308	1.8	153	0.9	171	1.0	923	5.4
1980	351	2.0	347	2.0	140	0.8	172	1.0	1010	5.8
1981	382	2.2	343	2.0	153	0.9	178	1.0	1056	6.2
1982	416	2.5	313	1.9	128	0.8	168	1.0	1025	6.1
1983	429	2.6	256	1.6	107	0.7	149	0.9	941	5.7
1984	496	3.0	340	2.1	119	0.7	154	0.9	1109	6.7
1985	517	3.2	365	2.3	106	0.7	143	0.9	1131	7.0
1986	554	3.4	341	2.1	109	0.7	167	1.0	1171	7.3
1987	616	3.8	334	2.1	127	0.8	184	1.1	1261	7.7
1988	634	3.9	300	1.8	136	0.8	210	1.3	1280	7.8
1989	683	4.0	278	1.6	127	0.8	245	1.5	1333	7.9
1990	709	4.3	252	1.5	134	0.8	261	1.6	1356	8.1
1991	695	4.3	244	1.5	152	0.9	323	2.0	1414	8.8
1992	666	4.1	265	1.6	161	1.0	335	2.1	1427	8.8
1993	731	4.4	347	2.0	191	1.1	378	2.3	1647	9.9
1994	791	4.7	372	2.2	229	1.4	422	2.5	1814	10.7
1995	835	4.9	378	2.2	259	1.5	495	2.9	1961	11.5
1996	899	5.2	403	2.3	286	1.6	546	3.1	2134	12.3
1997	894	5.2	391	2.3	321	1.8	590	3.4	2196	12.7
1998	970	5.5	431	2.4	363	1.9	610	3.4	2344	13.2
1999	918	5.2	462	2.6	306	1.7	577	3.3	2263	12.8
2000	904	5.2	475	2.9	265	1.5	563	3.2	2208	12.7
2001	955	5.3	542	3.0	267	1.5	592	3.3	2356	13.1

Above data courtesy of Multicultural Student Services at Washington State University.

10. The establishment of Women's Studies

I am pleased to acknowledge the important work of my successor, Sam Smith, who provided the leadership in the recruitment of some of these leaders, for the establishment of some of the above programs, and for his general commitment to the multicultural character of WSU.

Campus Unrest: There is No End

Unfortunately, there is no end in sight for the two major reasons for campus unrest in the 1960s and 1970s, racism and war. The changes, listed previously, that were brought about as a consequence of the unrest that existed at that time, were, and still are, changes that helped make the WSU campus a more accepting place for multicultural students, staff and faculty. I believe that we can agree that much remains to be done.

The active college and university campuses in my era, and today for that matter, are always in a state of unrest. Dissatisfaction with "the way things are" is encouraged in the university as an organization. This is central to its mission. Managing conflict and change in creative and open ways, keeping the peace, while continuing to maintain a consensus of support of faculty, students, regents, alumni and state officials are necessary for the president to continue to be effective.

The president cannot be effective if he or she makes decisions driven primarily by the effect of decisions on his/her job security. In fact, I think that university presidents should give more thought to the question of how long she or he can continue to be an effective leader in the office of the presidency. The job should seek the president in the first place, and the position should seek to retain the president. In other words, the president should be willing to resign at any time.

Some of the remaining chapters in this book will be treated as campus unrest, different from the 1960s and 1970s only in intensity and duration. Examples are the chapter on the explosion of Mt. St. Helens, intercollegiate athletics, and Butch, the university mascot.

1967
The beginning of the
24-hour days .

1985
After 18 years of
24-hour days.

Current WSU
President Lane and
wife Mary Jo Rawlins

Wallis Beasley,
Interim-President,
Executive Vice President
and my close advisor

Note left in my SeaTac Hyatt hotel room before my first meeting with WSU Alumni leaders in Vancouver, WA the next day.

The Regents responsible for my being hired as WSUs President, otherwise an unbelievably capable and amiable group. Standing left to right: Hal Romberg, Howard Morgan, Lyle Neff, Mike Dederer, Frances Owen; Seated left to right: Yours Truly, H. Dewayne Kreager, Dutch Hayner.

Governor and US Senator Dan Evans, the best governor I ever worked with — A great friend of higher education.

Gen DeVleming,
splendid assistant to myself
and four other presidents.
(Left and below)

Sally Savage, my capable
lawyer and assistant.

Lewis McNew,
Professor of English
and superb advisor
on student activism.

Dr. Lois DeFleur,
Dean of Arts and Science
and current President of
Binghamton University,
State University of NY

Dr. Rom Markin,
Dean of Business
and Economics

Warren A. Bishop,
Vice President
of Business

V. Lauren Shelton,
Vice President
of Finance

Art McCartan,
excellent Student Affairs officer

Al Yates, Provost
Currently President of Colorado
State University

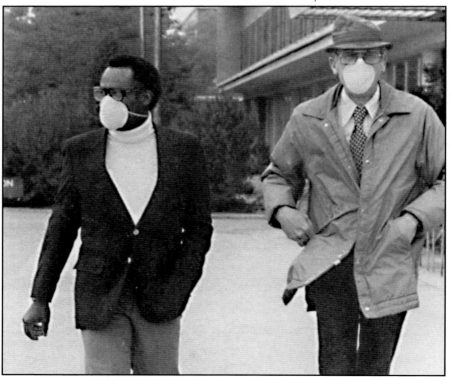

Terrell and Provost John Slaughter follow the advice about masks after the
eruption of Mt. St. Helens.

The Terrell Family, daughter Francie, son Glenn III and Francine.

The Bentley and friends

President Terrell's House Staff 1985
Row One: Lesley Davis, Carol Dambrosio, June Gillette (cook and hostess, president's residence), Roger Bolden. **Row Two:** Jenny Munizza, Gina Jausuro, Mary Ellen Walsh, Mary Warner, Pamela Barron, Janice Cohse, Colleen Jacot, Kelly Craig, Dina Company Curtis. **Row Three:** Marlene Counsell, Kim Morse, Curt Froland, Cliff Curtis.

Bea Taylor: talented housekeeper of "the residence." Anthropologist, fun to have around, bright and saucy.

Front and inside of a hand drawn card sent to me by students after Mt. St. Helens deposited ash on us and created havoc for about two weeks. Great example of Cougar humor!

Phil and June Lighty
Wonderful alumni, friends and
extraordinarily generous donors.

Tomas Ybarra (left) Dean of Student Affairs and Ron Taplin (right)
Assoc. Dean of Students, both at Bellevue Community College,
were leaders of Hispanic and African-American students.

(L to R) Matt Wanchena, Ky Tecumseh, myself, December 1995.
Two loyal WSU alumni friends

With a truly great Alumnus,
Weldon "Hoot" Gibson.

Les Purce, Ph.D.,
President, Evergreen College and
excellent advisor to Student Affairs.

Margarita Mendoza de Sugiyama,
Director of Consumer Services,
Washington State Office of
Attorney General, was a leader
within the Hispanic group.

Ernest L. Thomas, Ph.D.
President, Tarrant County College,
South Campus and a leader
of the African-American
students at WSU.

(L to R) President of Graduate and
Professional Student; Connie Kravas;
and Phyllis Campbell, Regent
and Alumna

Connie Kravas
Vice President University Relations,
President of WSU Foundation

Dr. Brian Benzel
Student leader during the activism and current
superintendent of Spokane Public Schools.

Members of the National Academy of Sciences, Engineering and Institute of Medicine

John Slaughter, National Academy of Engineering.

Clarence A. Ryan, Plant Biology.

Leo Bustad, National Institute of Medicine.

Linda L. Randall, Biochemistry

Diter von Wettstein, Plant Biology

John P. Hirth, Applied Physical Sciences

R. James Cook, Plant Pathology

Rodney B. Croteau, Institute of Biological Chemistry

Before discussing other events, it may be helpful to you for me to dwell a bit on what I consider to be the factors that enabled me to succeed in managing the student activism period, and to be among those invited to the Wingspread Conference. I trust that you will excuse me if I sound self-serving. I've intentionally waited 17 years to write this book, to give me a better perspective than I may have had immediately upon my retirement in 1985.

One does not survive as president of a major university without a great deal of help from others. In the early years, my close associates in the administration included Wallis Beasley, Executive Vice President; Jim Short, Dean of the Graduate School; Warren Bishop, Vice President Business; Loren Shelton, Vice President Finance; Gen DeVleming, my assistant; Jack Nyman, Dean of the Graduate School; the academic deans Art McCartan, Dean of Men and Jack Clevenger, Dean of Students. Several faculty members, including Lew McNew, professor of English; Rom Markin, professor of Business and chair of the faculty executive committee; and Vic Bhatia, Director of the Honors Program come to mind immediately.

Then there were leaders in the faculty, who organized a system for guarding the college and department facilities. The students who organized the assembling of students to attend the rallies to vote down any destructive suggestions were vital. The leadership skills exhibited by Nola Cross, the Editor of the student newspaper, The Evergreen, who chaired the rallies, and insisted that votes be taken on all the suggestions for demonstrations must be mentioned. And certainly Denny Morrison, my assistant, who maintained close contact with students and faculty members, was helpful.

Previously, I alluded to the importance of my relationships with students in my being among the successful survivors of the student unrest of the late 1960s and early 1970s. I spent much time with them, on campus, in their living units and in the student leaders' offices in the Student Union. I made it a point to get acquainted with them, to learn their names and their opinions of the Washington State University experience, of what they liked as well as what they did not understand or disliked. I found them to be very direct and honest in their responses. Most important, I learned first-hand of their affection for WSU, and about their family members, many of whom attended WSU.

Most of these students deserved to be trusted and respected. I gave them trust and respect. They were, and many still are, my friends. They were why the rest of us were there. They would soon be the leaders of the next generation. They invited me to their living units, dormitories and apartments for lunch and dinner, and I accepted those invitations because they were informative, interesting and enjoyable. They provided me with an opportunity to learn about their opinions on a myriad of issues related to what was happening at the university. In short, I learned that WSU students were different from those at any of the other colleges and universities I had previously known. I find, on the occasional visits I have with currently enrolled students, that they have the same charming, engaging manner and love for their school. Surely, some of them occasionally behave badly, break rules, and need to be disciplined. That just proves that they are subject to the same human frailties that on occasion afflict us all.

In summary, it is my belief that because of the immediate high priority I gave to getting acquainted with students, faculty, and administrative staff that I was prepared by those contacts to handle the peacekeeping responsibilities of the presidency. Although there were some colleagues who disagreed with some of the decisions that were made, as mentioned earlier, a university is a place were disagreement is not only tolerated, but invited. I mention this characteristic often because I believe it to be crucial to the understanding of decisions that we made during those troubled times.

Another factor in my surviving the campus capers was my willingness to "face the music" of my critics. The lecture tours we made immediately after the demonstrations proved to be crucial to my survival. Also important was my refusal to believe that the verbal attacks of the demonstrators and others were aimed at me personally. My patience, sense of humor, and the fact that I had no fear of and no anger toward the students certainly helped. I cite the following incident that demonstrated the absence of fear.

One evening around ten o'clock the doorbell rang, as it frequently did day or night. I went to the door, opened it and there was a huge man. I later learned he was six feet seven and weighed 300 pounds. He told me that he had heard that I needed a bodyguard. I looked up at him and said that I did not believe that I did, but that if I ever felt that I did need one, he would be the man I wanted for the job. I learned later that this man was working on his doctorate in the college of Education. He completed this program and is now on the staff of a community college in Los Angeles. For many years we exchanged letters. His name is Larry Jarmon.

I also kept the regents well-informed about what was going on and how and why we were attempting to handle these issues. Their support was essential, and it was unfailing. Some of them sometimes disagreed with my decisions, which is certainly understandable. But not one of them failed to support me, not only during campus unrest but throughout my tenure. Finally, I was fortunate. Many unfortunate things happen to university presidents through no fault of their own.

Other Causes of Contentious Demonstrations

Thus far, only brief reference has been made to the underlying causes of campus upheaval. We know that at WSU, racism and the Vietnam War triggered the protests. True, I cannot think of more serious illnesses of a society than racism and war. There are no more degrading problems than these. They wound the spirit of a nation. But why the 1960s and 1970s? What were the conditions then that generated the involvement of hundreds of thousands of students and many faculty members on many campuses and in cities, throughout the United States and in some foreign countries? Certainly, the Vietnam War was unpopular, not only with young men of draft age, but eventually with the majority of Americans. Thoughtful, fair-minded and empathetic people abhor racism.

But again, why the 1960s and the 1970s? In attempting to answer this question, I shall briefly describe some of the experiences of William McGill the Chancellor of the University of California at San Diego. Chancellor McGill was besieged by campus activism after he was appointed chancellor and even before he was inaugurated. No university president or chancellor experienced more difficult problems than he did, unless it was Roger Heyns, the Chancellor of the Berkeley campus. It all began at Berkeley with the Free Speech Movement in 1965, and included the terrifying riot over the People's Park, a dispute over the use of a plot of land. The university planned to use the land for married students' residences, while the protestors insisted that it remain a park for homeless and radical demonstrators.

McGill had the challenging experience of several revolts, one after the other in 1968 and 1969. The demonstrations involved at least three nationally known leaders of the student activism era: Eldridge Cleaver, information leader of the Black Panther party, and author of *Soul on Ice*; Herbert Marcuse, a Marxist social philosopher and a leader of the so-called New Left; and activist Angela Davis, a graduate student in philosophy. Also, just as difficult were the American Legion of San Diego, and Ronald Reagan, then-governor of California.

The Eldridge Cleaver story centered on whether or not Cleaver would be appointed to deliver a series of lectures entitled Social Analysis 139X. The Marcuse issue turned on whether or not Marcuse would have his appointment extended for another year. Angela Davis was an active participant in demonstrations on the campus. Given Reagan's conservative leadership style and political convictions, it was predictable that he and his Board of Regents appointees (about half of the members at that time) would take a hard line approach, including the use of police, with activists and leaders of the New Left.

McGill describes the disputes, demonstrations and attempts to resolve the differences between warring campus groups and the governor and regents in ways that would retain the traditional independence of the campus groups and be acceptable, if not ideal, to both groups. McGill was masterful. His book, *The Year of the Monkey,* is interesting reading to anyone, and especially relevant to those who will manage an institution of higher education in times of turmoil. His book alone is worth all the expense and time required by the Wingspread Conference and its participants.

The San Diego American Legion got wind of the consideration being given to a post-retirement appointment of one year for Professor Marcuse. They sent a letter strongly protesting the appointment of Marcuse. Somewhat surprisingly, the Regents delegated the decision to the chancellor, thus leaving the authority for such a decision with campus leaders. I have been brief with this issue. In fact, there were several weeks, including a number of demonstrations, before the issue was settled. McGill succeeded in convincing all involved that university procedures, with respect to the reappointment of professor Marcuse, be invoked. Again the persuasive skills of Chancellor McGill solved a serious conflict and preserved the independence of the university in matters of educational policy. I regard McGill and Roger Heyns, the Chancellor of the Berkeley campus during the activism era, as heroes among my generation of psychologists and university leaders.

I return to the question of the social, psychological and political forces that made campus revolts possible in the 1960s and 1970s, a question that has been discussed at length by many authors. Chancellor McGill himself devotes considerable space to this question in *The Year of the Monkey*. Unfortunately, there are still, and probably always will be, some variables that we may never fully understand. However, it is important that we grapple with this question, since the better we understand the answers the more effectively we will be in dealing with future revolts, which are sure to come.

We can conclude with confidence that at least seven factors, other than the obvious ones of the Vietnam War and racism, contributed to the unrest:

1. *Radicals of the New Left*. Although I remember some of the activists mentioned, like Eldridge Cleaver, Angela Davis, Bobby Seal and Tom Hayden, I saw no indication that our group had any direct connections with them. I remember them as simply having a mission of improving conditions for ethnic minority people. Besides, what would it take to get these leaders to Pullman? Berkeley, San Diego, Cornell - yes. But Pullman? No. We

did hear rumors of off-campus groups from Seattle, but I don't remember any evidence that they were at WSU.

2. *Interference by the governor and the Regents.* Classic examples of political interference occurred in California. Governor Reagan was running for re-election and, of course, took a hard line toward the activism on the campuses in the California higher education system. He also appointed to the Board of Regents people of like mind. Temperate leaders like Heyns and McGill had a difficult time making decisions without first getting the approval of the Board. What a difficult position for a campus leader to be in! Washington's Governor Dan Evans, as mentioned earlier, was a pillar of strength. Unlike other governors, he placed his confidence in the regents and the president to be equal to the most difficult assignment. Our Board of Regents basically delegated responsibility to the president. Also, as mentioned earlier, I kept the regents informed and listened carefully to their suggestions. Of course, sometimes things moved too fast for me to inform them until after the fact.

3. *Use of police.* Most of the campuses that called in the police to quell demonstrations simply made matters worse. The most frequently reported scenes where police were involved were Kent State University and Jackson State University where several students were killed. At WSU, we never considered calling police from other cities, thinking there wasn't anything about our problems that was worth risking the life of a single person. We had a unique situation, with a campus police force consisting of no more than a dozen officers, and not that many on duty at any one time. We had to talk our way through our problems or call in police reinforcements from off-campus, which we knew to be very risky.

4. *Poor communications between campus groups.* Several of the Study Councils reported communications difficulties, particularly between students, administration and faculty members. I have to believe that this was a chronic problem, not only at WSU, but on campuses generally. I believe that many students felt isolated, and still do. In fact, some told me so in our numer-

ous conversations. I also heard this feeling from faculty members, mostly in the context of a discussion about the remoteness of the administration, the so-called "ivory tower" concept. My awareness of this feeling influenced me in my determination to be accessible.

5. *Favorable economic times* of the 1960s and 1970s may have created a feeling in students that they had time to devote to idealistic programs and to protest the lack of idealism in all human institutions, including colleges and universities. If this was true, we would have expected some of them to be taken in by the more radical members of the New Left. I do not believe that the idealism of young people of college age is bad. Quite the contrary, I believe any society needs idealistic leaders. John Gardner was certainly an idealist. The leaders in the establishment of the independence of the United States and those who have contributed most to our nation's history like Washington, Jefferson, Lincoln and Martin Luther King were all driven by a dream of what this new nation could be. Likewise, the future of our country will be determined by modern idealistic heroes currently enrolled in our colleges and universities.

6. *The job market.* Some observers of the era of activism believe that support for the idealism theory explained in item 5 above is reinforced by the fact that the students today, during difficult economic times, are primarily interested in preparing themselves to compete for jobs.

7. *The military draft* at the time of the unpopular war in Vietnam contributed to activism. The re-instituting of the draft could be a contributing factor in the future.

In this book I am doing my best to present an unbiased appraisal of my performance. I have and will continue to mention mistakes I made, and some lost opportunities. As mentioned earlier, one of the most troubling was my failure to devote as much time and attention to faculty members who were not enthusiastic about, what appeared to them, to be my over-emphasis on research and graduate education, a major thrust of my vision for the future. I could have worked with them more effectively in an effort to convince them that teaching is just as important as research and the rewards for outstanding teaching are just as great as those for excellence in research.

At the same time, I want to recognize that, in general, my colleagues on the faculty were very supportive. They were particularly helpful during the activism period, as evidenced by the letter, written by 35 faculty members, quoted earlier. At the same time, I received some letters critical of the way I handled events on campus, usually from those who thought that I was not tough enough with the activists.

To me, no event was more important, in conveying a sense of appreciation for the way I handled the campus unrest, than the standing ovation the students gave me at the 1970 Commencement exercises. It was not due to my speech. I don't know of another university president who received that particular demonstration of support by students at the height of the student activism era. As good as it made me feel, it tells me more about the students than it does about me.

Chapter Four

THE ESTABLISHMENT OF THE WSU FOUNDATION

Very soon after I arrived on the WSU campus in 1967, I began to discuss the need for a foundation. I had been at the University of Illinois where a foundation had been bringing in millions of dollars a year for many years, for the support of academic programs. I soon discovered that the idea struck fear in some of the colleges and departments. They were concerned that a foundation would absorb their efforts to raise funds for their departments and that they would lose the relatively few donors they had recruited over the years. The campus leaders initially were uniformly negative, and, of course, their support was essential to the success of the Foundation. It was necessary for me to convince them to believe that the Foundation would greatly increase their support from donors.

I also began approaching corporations, other foundations and some individual prospective donors about the idea. I was met with a generally cool response, especially in my discussions with business and foundation leaders. Their view was that since public universities are supported by the legislature, their support would continue for private institutions of higher education. We responded to that by pointing out that legislative appropriations for public universities fell far short of our total budgetary needs, and that donations to public universities would raise the level of awareness of the need of additional funds in both the public and private institutions.

The discussions with campus leaders continued. Even though we were still consumed with managing the campus activism and maintaining the peace, we did not let the idea drop. We believed that if deans and department heads became aware of the success of foundations in other universities in the nation and the benefits departments received from an organized and aggressive foundation, they would support the idea. Acting on that assumption, in 1970 we appointed Keith Cluckey, a person from the University of Southern California who had worked in the successful development office of that institution, to work with us in establishing the feasibility of later formally creating a Foundation.

Unfortunately, Mr. Cluckey's appointment did not work out. After about a year, he accepted a similar appointment at Gonzaga University. Keith was succeeded in 1977 by Doug Kinsey, from the UCLA Development Office. Doug remained in the position as Director of Development until we appointed Connie Kravas as Executive Director in 1980. In 1981, the additional title, President of the Foundation was added. The huge success of the WSU Foundation is due largely to the superb performance of Connie. She had the intelligence, personal skills, commitment, and energy that the position requires. She is now showing our friends at the University of Washington how a development office works. Our new Vice President for Development, Rick Frisch has the experience and the necessary personal skills for good leadership. We owe him the support he will need to be successful.

Table Two (on the following page) contains data demonstrating the increasing success of the WSU Foundation since its formal inception, beginning in 1978 through 1985, coinciding with my tenure. I include 2002 in order to present the donations for that year and the total for the history of the Foundation, an astonishing figure of $636 million.

I have gone into some detail explaining that, informally, the

Table Two			
Contributions to WSU Foundation: 1978–1985; 2002			
Year	Gifts	Grants	Total
1967	496,363		496,363
1968	319,603		319,603
1969	450,845		450,845
1970	403,139		403,139
1971	417,538		417,538
1972	754,007		754,007
1973	1,243,342		1,243,342
1974	913,736		913,736
1975	892,215		892,215
1976	1,054,602		1,054,602
1977	2,006,484		2,006,484
1978	1,070,195	3,263,833	4,334,028
1979	1,867,418	3,559,159	5,426,577
1980	2,208,000	4,100,707	6,308,707
1981	2,178,617	4,850,064	7,028,681
1982	2,476,069	5,272,485	7,748,554
1983	4,273,626	5,497,606	9,771,232
1984	5,670,634	5,233,032	10,903,666
1985	6,771,726	5,770,453	12,542,179
2002	8,605,292	14,133,767	42,739,059

Grand Total: 636,699,727

private fundraising effort began with Keith Cluckey's appointment in 1970. Much necessary work was done before the date of its formal establishment in 1979. This included the appointment of a Visiting Committee, whose expertise and dedicated work was so essential to the soundness of the structure of the Foundation and its relationship with the university and the Board of Regents. The Visiting Committee was chaired by Weldon G. "Hoot" Gibson, a Distinguished Alumnus with a long history of generous support to WSU. He was later elected the Founding Chair of the Foundation. What a guy he was! What a multitude of talents! Bright, sneaky bright, in fact! What a sense of humor! What a generous soul! And he was the only person I ever knew who could sleep through a speech and know more than anybody else about what the speaker had said. The other members of the Visiting Committee were Vice Chair, Regent H. Dewayne Kreager, an intensely loyal WSU alumnus, and one of the all-time most talented leaders responsible for the rapid development of the Puget Sound area in the 1950-1990 decades; and three other loyal alumni, J.L. Lemery, Treasurer; K.B. Myklebust, Secretary and P. McKevitt.

Jay Rockey, a prominent alumnus from Seattle, has been an effective leader in the WSU Foundation from the beginning. Recently, he received the highest honor the Foundation recognizes, The Weldon "Hoot" Gibson award. Jay has been an outstanding force in the Northwest's advertising and public relations industry for forty years.

In addition to Connie, I express my appreciation to Sam Smith for his strong support of the Foundation. I add to this my belief that the Foundation will be even more successful during Lane Rawlins' tenure. He made a public statement recently that got my attention. Following comments about the importance of increased support from the legislature, Lane expressed great confidence and hope for the future by saying, in effect, that we will succeed in reaching our goals, primarily because of our belief in our own resourcefulness. Much research has been performed by social-cognitive theorists showing the power of individual and collective belief. I was glad to hear this in President Rawlins' comments. In retrospect, I did too much hand-wringing and agonizing about legislative support, and not enough about instilling individual and organizational belief.

After the Foundation was established, my schedule changed dramatically. Approximately half of my time was spent fund raising, if relationships with the legislature are included. And as the success of the Foundation increased, my time supporting the Foundation increased. One very important point needs to be made. There was a precursor of a foundation inherent in the Scholarship Development Program of the Alumni Association, initiated by Pat Patterson, in so many ways one of the more prominent Cougars ever. Some of the colleges also had their own fundraising programs. The establishment of the WSU Foundation centralized the fund raising effort, while providing professional assistance to the colleges and departments. The result of its creation, of course, greatly increased the donations to the colleges and departments. But let us not forget the importance of those who were raising money through donations many years earlier.

The Stadium Project

The first major fund raising efforts of my tenure involved securing gifts to rebuild the south stands of the football stadium at the Rogers Field site. As a matter of fact, this campaign began in 1972, well before the formal establishment of the Foundation. The success of this campaign demonstrated that the time was right for the establishment of a WSU Foundation.

An alumnus from Spokane, Wes McLaughlin, suggested that we talk with the wealthy son of a former Washington governor, Clarence Martin. The son, Dan Martin, was a very successful businessman in Los Angeles. I called him and asked for an appointment to discuss his interest in Washington State University. He had spent some time in eastern Washington in his early years, since Governor Martin was a resident of Cheney, Washington. He was a very polite man who agreed to meet with me when WSU played Southern California in Los Angeles.

I invited Ray Nagel, our Director of Athletics and two of our Regents, Harold Romberg and Lyle Neff, to accompany us to meet Mr. Martin. We also invited Mr. and Mrs. Martin to a dinner, at the home of a relative of the Nagels, after our meeting in Mr. Martin's office. All of these arrangements were made a few weeks in advance of the game in Los Angeles.

The plan for rebuilding the south stands included an academic facility, with the Computer Science department to be under the stands. We thought that combination would increase the attractiveness of the facility, in view of reports that Mr. Martin was interested in academics as well as athletics. He was a part-owner and vice president of the Los Angeles Rams NFL football team. He also had earned a Masters degree from Harvard, not that it necessarily had anything to do with his success as a business man.

As the time approached for our meeting, I became increasingly apprehensive about how I was to put the question to Mr. Martin. After all, this was to be my first effort to secure a major gift. The cost of rebuilding the south stands of the stadium was a million dollars. The plan was to ask him for a quarter of a million, and in return we would name the stadium for his father. It seemed rather crude to simply ask him for that much money without having met the man, and without knowing his feelings about the State of Washington or WSU. These thoughts led me to do some research on the Martin family. I discovered that Governor Martin frequently visited the WSU campus as the guest of President Holland. The governor apparently supported WSU in his position as governor. I found out also that there was no building or other facility named for the governor. It seemed strange to me that a two-term governor of our state, who had a good reputation of public service, had not been memorialized in some significant way. With this background of facts, I began to feel comfortable with the thought that the governor's son just may find the naming of our stadium for his father very attractive.

The meeting in Mr. Martin's office in Los Angeles went well. The two regents and Ray Nagel accompanied me, and our prospect was very cordial and warm, but understandably made no commitment at that time. Ray and Shirley Nagel and the evening's host and hostess had a great dinner and the stage was beautifully set for a more serious and direct conversation about the stadium. The Martins said the offer was appreciated and that they would give it serious thought. Their interest was palpably greater than during our afternoon meeting with Mr. Martin. I am indebted to the Nagels for making this possible. The setting could not have been more conducive to an affirmative response, which came several weeks later.

Mr. Martin accepted our offer on New Years Eve, 1972. I found it possible to be in Los Angeles on that day, and we had a celebratory drink. The only person more pleased than I was Dan. (By that time we were on a more personal basis.) I have found it to be true that most decisions to give to the university are not primarily financial ones. Rather it is an act from the heart. That is the single most important lesson I learned from the Martin association. The preparations we made were designed to touch the heart, and it worked. Charlotte Martin later gave a substantial amount toward the expansion of the north side of the stadium, before Father Coughlin, President of Gonzaga at that time, replaced WSU as number one in her heart. I console myself with the thought that the Father probably had the Lord on his side. It could not have happened to a nicer person, even though the good Father's gain was our loss. Obviously, our traditional defeat by the USC Trojans did not put the "kabosh" on the deal. (We beat them more often now, I am happy to report.)

Chapter Five

THE ROLE OF
INTERCOLLEGIATE ATHLETICS

As is the case with all chapters of this book, my treatment of intercollegiate athletics is from the perspective of the president's office. For those readers interested in a complete historical picture of the athletic programs at WSU, I refer them to the excellent Centennial book written by Dick Fry, *The Crimson and the Gray*, published by WSU Press.

You will notice that, in this book, more attention is given to football than to other sports programs. The simple reason for that is the demands made on the president's office with respect to football far exceeds those of other sports programs. From a purely personal standpoint, my interest in competitive sports programs was driven by student-athletes' interests, not by the attendance or financial figures. Support for that view appears in the next part of this book.

Women's Programs

Before Title IX, there were relatively few intercollegiate sports for women at WSU. One reason for that was the apparent lack of interest by women athletes for additional programs. Perhaps I should have been more aware than I was of a need that was developing. That is not like me, nor is it like my associates. As mentioned earlier, the financial problems of immediately supporting the developing interests of women athletes in intercollegiate sports were huge. But that is history. It is my understanding that there is equal opportunity now. I must confess that the performance of women athletes has greatly exceeded my expectations in many sports, particularly in basketball and golf. Enough of my expectations. The fact is that educators and psychologists are prone to underestimate the limits of human performance, women and men, in many areas, both physical and mental.

Football

Competitive sports have always been important at WSU, as it is at most major research universities in our country, public and private. I had been an interested observer of sports programs at all of the universities and colleges with which I had been affiliated.

WSU is a member of the Pac-10 Conference, and before that, the Pac-8 Conference. The Pac-10 Conference is comprised of the major research universities on the West Coast, including, besides us, Washington, Oregon, Oregon State, Stanford, California Berkeley, University of Southern California, UCLA, Arizona and Arizona State. Membership in this conference is important academically. And like it or not (and I do), the general public sees it that way. Although propinquity plays a role in determining conference membership, so does similarity of mission. Little did I know that conference membership would be a major factor for what I would call "former student" or alumni activism during my first year at WSU.

We were playing Stanford University in Palo Alto in the fall of 1967. I traveled with the team to the Bay area for the game and a meeting for the first time with California alumni. One of the best memories I have of game day was the interview with Keith Jackson, who, because of his prominence as a sports announcer, was one of my heroes. My elation with this experience quickly turned sour. We lost the game, but it was the explanation of our football coach, Bert Clark, about why we lost that was disturbing to me. He questioned our kids' courage. That was bad. Even worse, for the university and our competitive sports program, he gratuitously questioned the appropriateness of our membership in the then Pac-8 Conference. Questioning the courage of athletes may be considered an issue between the coach and his or her student-athletes. I didn't like it because I thought it was offensive to our student-athletes. But questioning the broader policy decision as to conference membership was clearly out of his domain of authority.

There was a ground swell of protests by alumni. By the time I arrived back in Pullman, there were many telephone messages from students, alumni, Cougar Club members, and even from some regents, who themselves had been deluged with calls. The anger was about equally focused on the coach's labeling our squad cowards as his statement about our membership in the Pac-8 Conference. Many of the protestors wanted me to fire the coach immediately. Even a few regents wanted immediate action. Since we were approaching the end of the season, I thought it best to wait until the season was over, and I persuaded the regents to go along with that plan. Most of the alumni accepted that decision, probably not wanting to force the issue in the new president's first year on the job. That was a typical reaction of the alumni at WSU. They were, and still are, marvelous people, and were among my strongest supporters the entire time I was at WSU. They are, after all, former students, and remain among my best friends.

Before I conclude my treatment of this, my first experience with activism in our sports programs, I want to say that the coach took the news of his impending replacement like the professional person that he was. He seemed to understand, and seemed not in the least angry or resentful toward the university.

The recruitment of Clark's successor was the first of five football coaches we recruited during my tenure. That must be a national record. Jim Sweeney, the expansive, charming Irishman, was the next football coach. He and his family arrived early in the new year of 1968, somewhat late to be totally prepared for the all-important recruiting of new football talent. Coach Sweeney was at WSU for eight years through the 1975 season. His teams performed quite well in the first two or three years, and then not so well for a year or two. In fact, other Pac-8 schools began to dominate us in ways that Jim was unaccustomed to. He invited Lou Tice, founder and chairman of The Pacific Institute, to spend a few days with his squad to instruct them in goal-setting and other cognitive skills that would enhance performance. Mr. Tice had developed an excellent reputation for working with educational, corporate and public agencies, as well as athletic organizations, with programs designed to assist them in achieving the best performance of which they are capable. (I mentioned my association with the Tices and The Pacific Institute earlier in the introduction, while describing my post-WSU life. More on this in a later chapter.)

Following Lou Tice's work with the football squad, the team began to win. In my conversations with the football players, during my many walks on the campus, I found them to be most enthusiastic about what they had learned from the concepts Lou Tice had taught them, particularly the stimulating power of goal-setting and its value in enhancing performance on and off the field.

Some readers may question my including a chapter on athletics. Any president of a major Division I-A university (those major research universities with large stadiums) knows of the importance of competitive sports. It is important to the president because of its importance to most of the university's constituents: Students, current and former; state officials; and the business communities. If the Cougars are winning, the emotional tone is upbeat; if they are losing, it's down-beat. Let's face it, upbeat people are more supportive. Many students in western states want to attend Pac-10 schools. Interest in athletics often leads to interest in academic programs. Donors are more likely to give to universities with Foundations, with gifts earmarked for departments and disciplines of their choice.

Back to the Sweeney era. Jim's recruiting skills enabled him to persuade some of the best talent in the state of Washington to attend WSU. He was beginning to compete successfully against the "flagship university." (I admire that university, but despise that metaphor.) In 1975, Jim had his heart set on winning the Pac-8 conference and taking his team to the Rose Bowl. His chances dimmed when California beat us toward the end of that season. The next day he came to the president's home to tell me that he was resigning after the season. I tried to persuade him not to resign, that he had brought the team to a level where he could compete for the championship each year, and winning would probably come soon. Unfortunately, he did not change his mind. He went on to establish a winning record at Fresno State University. It pleases me that Fresno State recently named the stadium for him. Jim Sweeney, along with Jim Walden and Mike Price have, along with the immortal Babe Hollingberry of an earlier era, contributed immensely to the Cougar Spirit. Dennis Erickson had the skills and football knowledge to be in the same class. Unfortunately, his tenure was too short to be included in the same foursome named above.

Jim Walden was another colorful and successful coach. He was particularly adept at beating teams with superior talent. He had the knack of getting his team ready for a big game. But nothing, nor anyone, is perfect. He, like all coaches, university presidents, and the rest of us, on occasion had the "knack" of losing the ones we were suppose to win. Jim had more success than I can recall in beating the UW Huskies than most of his predecessors or successors, much to the delight of all Cougars. And, he was greatly pursued by the sports writers for his directness and his sense of humor.

Jim Walden and Jim Sweeney and their families remain good friends of my family members and me. I shall never forget the phone call I received from Jim Walden when it became known that we would be in our first Rose Bowl in 60-plus years, in which he told me that I had helped lay the groundwork for the production of a winning football program at WSU. Thank you, Jim. So did you.

Mike Price, like the two "Jims," (Sweeney and Walden) is just right for WSU. He quickly identified with Cougar traditions, alumni and Cougar boosters. He has a great sense of humor, a tremendous asset to football coaches and university presidents.

Although I was not president when Mike was head football coach, I was there early in his career when he was an assistant coach with Jim Sweeney. Mike has the distinction of taking the Cougars to the Rose Bowl for the first time in more than 60 years.

Intercollegiate athletics provided me with the opportunity to become quite popular with the business community in Washington. We had a run on head football coaches when Jim Sweeney resigned. We had four coaches, including Sweeney, in as many years. Jackie Sherrill, for one year, Warren Powers for one year and Jim Walden who stayed for nine years. It was bad enough when Sherrill left after one year. But when Powers did the same, I reached the end of my patience. I was sick of recruiting coaches who left before fulfilling their contractual obligations. When we recruited Powers, we offered him and he accepted a three-year contract which contained a clause that required him to pay WSU the remaining obligation if he left before three years. He left after one year to return to his Alma Mater, the University of Missouri. I had called the president of the University of Missouri and told him that we would sue him and his university if Coach Powers left without paying the remaining two years of his contract with WSU. Powers paid for the two remaining years on his contract. Apparently, this was the first time this had been done in a major university. We not only got words of approval from many Washingtonians, but also from officials from other universities in the nation. I still do not understand the one-way obligation of coaches' contracts or any contracts including the President's. It is supposed to make sense, since the competition to keep winning coaches is so strong, but that doesn't make it right.

Basketball, Baseball and Track

The other major sports – basketball, baseball and track – were relatively free of campus activism during my tenure. However, as mentioned earlier, the purpose of this book is not entirely focused on how high levels of activism were managed successfully. I have three other reasons, or goals in mind, all of which are contained in the title of the book: ministry, heart and organizational theory. Whatever success I was able to experience as President of WSU during periods of high and low level activism, was due to these important concepts. I cannot write this book without giving credit to those who made it possible for me to contribute. Constructive leadership in universities requires effective teamwork, and we had a good team of very competent professionals who had the best interests of WSU at heart. Many colleagues will be identified. But regrettably, not all. Please forgive me for that.

Mention basketball at WSU and three names immediately come to mind – Jack Friel, Marv Harshman and George Raveling. Marv was the head coach when I came to WSU. We lost him to the University of Washington a few years later. Jack Friel is a Cougar legend, as is George Raveling. Need I say more? Yes. Although I was not at WSU in the Jack Friel era, I knew him well for many years. He was not only a superb coach, but an intellect as well. George Raveling, a great recruiter AND coach, was also an intellectual, one of the best read persons in his time at WSU. I capitalized the word "and" in writing about Coach Raveling because writers of WSU sports sometimes spoke of George as an excellent recruiter, neglecting to give him the praise he richly deserves for his coaching ability. He was also highly respected as a national leader in the sports world. George and I remain close friends. I give Ray Nagel, our athletic director at the time, credit for persuading George to come to WSU.

Baseball. WSU pretty much dominated baseball for most of Coach Bo-Bo Brayton's career, especially in the Northwest. He held his own in Southern California as well. He is mainly responsible for the baseball facilities at WSU, among the best not only in the Pac-10 conference, but in the nation. Bo-Bo is a legend too, along with his predecessor Buck Bailey, the colorful uncle of the also colorful Weldon "Hoot" Gibson, the founding Chairman of the WSU Foundation. Bo-Bo also handled the student activism era with intelligence and humor.

Track. Three coaches in WSU track programs during my tenure are Jack Moobery, John Chaplin, and the current coach, Rick Sloan. They cover more than 40 years. They were all exceptionally capable, won far more than they lost, were a power in the Pac-10 Conference and were competitive in the NCAA meets. The track facility was named for coach Mooberry in recognition of the quality of the teams he had over the years. John Chaplin gained national and international fame by recruiting outstanding athletes from several foreign countries.

Athletic directors have a difficult job. All of the directors we had were excellent. In addition to Ray Nagel, and Sam Jankovich, who I mentioned earlier, Stan Bates and Dick Young also represented WSU very effectively.

Chapter Six

ALUMNI-STUDENT RELATIONSHIPS

Alumni

The distinction between alumni and students is a difficult one. Many events involve both. I list these events involving alumni and students in the same chapter, but in different sections. Since alumni by definition graduated first, I include experiences, for the most part, involving alumni in the first part and those involving students in the second. But be forewarned, they will overlap. The Alumni Association Presidents during my tenure appear below in Table Three.

Table Three	
Alumni Association Presidents: 1967–1985	
1967 Herbert Hemingway	1977 Joe F. Caraher
1968 Barry K. Jones	1978 Stanley S. Pratt
1969 George D. Barclay	1979 David C. Abbott
1970 Donald C. Downen	1980 Richard Gustafson
1971 Robert C. Morgan	1981 Chellis (Smith) Swenson
1972 John "Jack" Sutherland	1982 Bruce Monroe
1973 Thomas L. Copeland	1983 Dennis McLaughlin
1974 Robert K. Lundgaard	1984 Stan Coe
1975 Howard A. Nessen	1985 Kevin Veleke
1976 William J. Biggar	

The alumni presidents who perhaps had the most difficult tenure were those whose fate it was to be the alumni leader during the campus demonstrations: Herb Hemingway, 1967; Barry Jones, 1968; George Barclay, 1969; Don Downen, 1970; Bob Morgan, 1971; and on a reduced scale, Jack Sutherland, 1972. Although, like me, these leaders didn't always understand the whys and whats about the campus unrest and what should have been done about them, they always supported me as president. Even though they may have, on occasion, disagreed with the way I managed things at their school, they were always patient with me.

I have a rather broad definition of alumni. They include those who earned a degree from WSU; those who attended WSU but did not graduate, but still consider themselves an alumnus or alumna; those with an honorary degree from WSU; and those who are honorary Cougars, like me, an honor that I cherish. In other words, being an alumna or alumnus of WSU, like being the president of WSU, is more of an affair of the heart than academic degrees. I know of no other university where I would define alumni in this way. My definition of a Cougar is anyone who is a member of a Cougar Club, with or without an academic history at WSU, but who wants to be affiliated and identified with our university, either through academics or sports. Or both.

My first experience with WSU students (now alumni) away from the campus, after I had arrived in Pullman, was in Seattle at the Hyatt Hotel near the airport. I had attended a meeting of a legislative committee, and spent the night at the motel where the meeting had been held. The next morning I had breakfast and returned to my room to gather my belongings, as I was on my way to meet with alumni leaders in Vancouver, Washington. I discovered a note from two WSU students that contained the following message, "Welcome to WSU. This is not Cougar country, but nothing is perfect." It was signed by, "Two Cougars working their way through school." What a warm greeting that was! I knew then that if these two students were representative of the student body, I had made the right decision to accept the presidency of WSU. The students left no name, but later I found out the name of one of them was Carol Lewis. My meeting the next day with the Alumni Association leaders in Vancouver added another element of certainty to my feeling about having joined the company of Cougars. Absolutely nothing ever happened after that to spoil that beginning, or to cause me to regret my decision.

The alumni of WSU are best described as loyal and passionate about their university. For the most part, they are constant in their support of each other and their school. They are fun-loving, warm-hearted, and low-key (except when they collectively have strong feelings about something like the new Alumni Center), or when someone is harsh in their criticism of WSU or a group representing WSU. Their loyalty kicks in under those circumstances when, for example, a coach questions the courage of his team of Cougar athletes.

An event occurred in the late 1970s which provides a window to the behavioral style of alumni and students – the death of Butch the mascot, during the annual meeting of the alumni leaders. It was first reported that Butch died of natural causes associated with old age. A later report revealed that Butch had been euthanized. Apparently, a student saw someone transporting Butch from his cage to the College of Veterinary Medicine, followed them to the College and discovered that Butch was, as the saying goes, "put down." Butch's demise became a big issue, among students and former students. After all, Butch had long been the Cougar mascot, the only one many of the living alumni had ever known.

What to do about this became a big issue, both on and off campus, which illustrates a comment made earlier that a university campus is constantly in a state of mild or wild unrest about academic, athletic or social issues. For several weeks, emotions were high over the question of whether or not we should replace Butch with another live cougar. The only organizational theory or management assumption we could apply to this issue was the concept of shared governance. This called for open communication with alumni and students and if they were interested, the faculty. We decided that the majority opinion would settle it, so we took a vote of the alumni leaders at the meeting, which turned out to be nearly unanimous in favor of another live cougar.

The students, anticipating that Butch would soon go the way of all living creatures (he *was* showing his age), had the foresight to place an item on the student body election ballot indicating their preference for a live cougar or a person dressed in a cougar costume. The live cougar tally was slightly higher than the fake cougar vote, something like 51% to 49%. This meant that the students and alumni leaders agreed. So, I happily announced that we would get a live cougar that had been born in captivity, and had no chance of ever being in the wild, for our new Butch. The animal rights group on campus immediately went to work, led by the students and faculty from the Veterinary College, who presented me with a petition, which was supported by the entire College, urging me to reverse the decision.

At this point, I decided to have a sack lunch meeting in the Student Service Center in the CUB to which all interested parties were invited. I needed more information. I got it. Many individuals told me that student opinions had changed following the vote on the election ballot, and that furthermore, that vote was not valid because so many students did not vote, as is frequently the case in student elections. At that point, we announced that the Social and Economic Science Research Center, which was established upon the recommendation of the Social Science Study Council, would conduct a scientific opinion survey of the student body on the Butch issue. The result of that survey indicated that student opinion was the reverse of the student election poll, i.e., about 60% for a costumed Butch, and 40% for a live cougar.

At this time, Keith Lincoln, Alumni Association Director, agreed that this was an issue that needed to be decided by the students. We then decided we would ask the Alumni Association leaders to yield to student wishes. They did. Keith did a good job of persuading them, and they were characteristically cooperative when they saw the bind we were in. It is important to add that most of those who wanted a live mascot accepted the students' decision as being fair. I must add that Bill Munro, an excellent alumnus from San Francisco, needled me in good humor about the decision, and continued to tell me that he would be shipping me a live cougar soon.

Some readers may think we took more time with this issue than it deserved. It was my experience that good insight about anticipating potentially serious problems on university campuses, and good judgment about the best way to handle potentially serious problems, are skills that help leaders perform their duties. I have noticed that issues associated with mascots on a number of university campuses can generate lengthy, emotionally-charged difficulties. Thankfully, due to the cooperative nature of WSU alumni, we avoided serious problems.

The Lewis Alumni Center

Several years before I retired, the Alumni Association became interested in an attractive facility on campus that would serve as a center of activity for the Association. Dennis McLaughlin, President of the Association at that time, along with Keith Lincoln, were the leaders of this effort. They had the strong and unanimous support of the Association members. Earlier, I characterized the WSU alumni as low-key, patient and easy-going except when they had a goal that was important to them, collectively. The Alumni Center is a striking example of what they can accomplish if they put their heart, mind and determination into a project. It is an elegant structure, which also exudes warmth. It is a modern facility which preserves the land-grant history and tradition of WSU. (It retains the original shape of a barn.) It is so inviting that the Board of Regents holds its meetings there, and it is a marvelous facility for social gatherings.

The $4 million dollar cost of the project did not phase the alumni, with Dennis at the helm. The alumni persuaded the WSU Foundation to assist in raising the money. It helped immensely to have Jack Lewis pledge a million dollars at the retirement party given for me in Pullman. I had no idea that he was going to do that. Perhaps he was "carried away" by the emotions of the moment. But my belief is that he had given some thought to it before the party. In any event, he made the gift, and quite appropriately, the building carries his name, which reminds me of my interest in how buildings on a university campus get named. In universities, the governing board makes the final decision about building names.

Universities differ in how and when these decisions are made, and who participates in the process. Some name buildings for individuals at any time the governing board desires. Others only after the individual to be honored is deceased. Still others name buildings after those who give generously, or those who have pledged to leave significant gifts in their will. At WSU, the trend is to give heavy weight to those who make generous current or deferred gifts, a policy that I strongly endorse. The reason is simply that the funding of higher education continues to drop. We are very close to being desperate. Some universities already are.

The disappointing part about all this is that the words regarding the importance of higher education from those running for public office too often do not match their priorities as expressed in their budgets after they are elected. The reason usually given is that these are tough economic times. It occurs to me that the importance of higher education is even greater when there is an economic downturn. Not enough political leaders are champions of higher education.

Getting back to building naming policies. In my opinion, we are desperate enough to adopt what may appear to some to be a crass way to name buildings, i.e., to name them for people who give substantial sums of money. It is not an ideal way to help solve our financial problems, but it makes good practical sense. Incidentally, I recognize that this is a departure from one of the main themes of this book, namely, that decisions should flow from a theoretical base. However, it is consistent with my observation that a major gift to a university is an act of the heart, not basically a financial transaction. So, a policy of naming buildings or programs for major donors stems from decisions of the heart by the donor.

Students

There are two sets of student leaders: undergraduates (ASWSU) and Associated Graduate Students. Graduate student leaders are not usually as active in student life, except in extraordinary times like campus unrest or whenever issues of particular importance to graduate students are being discussed. They are usually too busy with the demands of graduate work to become engrossed in most campus activities. The leaders that I worked with most often were the ASWSU presidents and vice-presidents and their assistants. Table Four (below) contains the names of the presidents and vice-presidents from 1967 to 1985, the years of my tenure.

Table Four
ASWSU Presidents & Vice-Presidents: 1967–1985

Year	President	Vice-President
1966-67	Tom Glover	Jim Camp
1967-68	Steve Kukuchi	Duncan Carter
1968-69	Ray Crabbs	Dave Cardwell
1969-70	Brian Benzel	Norm Davis
1970-71	Carlton Lewis	Scot Hendrickson
1971-72	Carlton Lewis	Chris Schlect
1972-73	Chris Schlect	Jim Boldt
1973-74	Paul Casey	Mike Sweeney
1974-75	Paul Casey	Richard Slunaker
1975-76	Linda Carlisle	Brian Jappert
1976-77	Roland Lewis	Bart Block
1977-78	Mark Ufkes	Greg King
1978-79	Tom Pirie	Van Snyder
1979-80	Gary Baker	Larry Clark
1980-81	John Winkler	Josh Pierce
1981-82	Rob Hoon	Dan Peterson
1982-83	Mike Morgan	Glenn Osterhout
1983-84	Dan O'Connell	Sara Roe
1984-85	Mike Coan	Jim Van Den Dysseel
1985-86	Dave Pridemore	Barbara Gorham

The activity levels of most of these leaders were very high. In fact, much more so than student leaders I have observed at any of the other six universities with which I have been connected as a student or faculty member. As one would expect, some were more active than others. Although some of these officers were more interested in the politics of the campus than others, I think the differences in the degree of their involvement were determined by the issues being discussed on the campus during their tenure and their general energy level.

Accordingly, Ray Crabbs, Brian Benzel, and Carlton Lewis (who had two terms), perhaps had the toughest leadership responsibilities because they were being pulled from every direction by student opinion regarding the war in Vietnam and racism. Gary Baker and John Winkler had the hysteria created by the potentially serious health consequences of the ash from Mt. St. Helens. Chris Schlect, Paul Casey (who also had two terms), Linda Carlisle and Roland Lewis, were active because of their strong interest in political and social issues of the campus. Mark Ufkes and Tom Pirie were active because of their exceptionally high energy level, and their interest in campus politics and the changes needed in our society, both on and off campus.

Rob Hoon, Mike Morgan, Dan O'Connell, Mike Coan and Dave Pridemore, even though there were no survival issues confronting the campus during their presidencies, were very active improving university policies regarding the students' role in university governance. One misunderstanding occurred between these officers and the Director of Athletics, Sam Jankovich, over changes in student seating in Martin Stadium. As is so often the case, the source of the difficulty was a breakdown in communication, for which I assume the responsibility. I do not believe Sam was opposed to student involvement in issues like this. He was attempting to modify the seating arrangement in order to maximize revenues. As I remember, the student officers were concerned more over the belief that they were not adequately consulted than their opposition to the changes in seating. Their complaint was supported by the fact that student activity fees contribute to the cost of athletics. Sam's job was to balance the Athletic Department's budget, a perennial problem at WSU. Incidentally, Sam Jankovich was as effective as any of my colleagues in accomplishing important goals. He lead the way in expanding Martin Stadium and Academic Center to what it is today.

The vice presidents were often as skilled as the presidents, and not surprisingly, in a few instances, superior. I enjoyed working with all of them. Each took their job seriously, and wanted to do what was best for their university. That is a remarkable fact. And I can say the same about other student leaders. The best example I can give was the alerting system students organized to vote down potentially destructive actions proposed during the demonstrations in the spring of 1970.

Student Involvement in Governance

Several important issues occurred on campus which gave me opportunities to involve students in university governance as an important part of their personal development.

The Student Radio Station

In the mid 1970s, I had a visit from two students, Christie DeJulio and Bill Stewart, who were requesting permission to establish a student operated radio station in the Compton Union Building. At first I had doubts about the wisdom of approving the request because of the potential for negative consequences. Nevertheless, I approved it and told them that I would recommend its approval by the regents. Christie and Bill were placed on the meeting agenda for a presentation of their proposal to the Regents. They made a very convincing case for the radio station. The regents, after expressing some of the same reservations that I had, approved it. The station was established and ever since has been managed very responsibly. In fact, shortly after the station began broadcasting, we had to contend with the ash of Mt. St. Helens. Contrary to the university operated station, KWSU, the student station invariably checked out rumors, which were rampant, before airing them. And in so doing, they helped avoid unnecessary fear on the campus. Bill Vadino was a capable manager of the student station during that time.

Drugs in the Beasley Coliseum

In another incident, some students began using drugs and alcohol at concerts in Beasley Coliseum. Mark Ufkes, ASWSU President at the time was given the responsibility of controlling this potentially explosive problem. Mark was a very conscientious president. It was a student problem, and we decided to give him the responsibility of controlling it. He designated students to attend the concerts with the responsibility of asking offending students to stop. It worked. Had we used police officers, the result could have been negative. Mark and the other student leaders, including Mark Elliott, who participated were deservedly proud of their accomplishment and I was of them. This is not a knock on WSU's police department. In fact, they did an excellent job. But sometimes the sight of a police officer's uniform incites fear or anger. Generally, our officers enjoyed the respect of students.

Libya

Mark Ufkes managed to get himself and me invited to visit Gaddafi, the Libyan leader, who at that time, the late 1970s, was suspected of supporting terrorists who had hijacked commercial airliners. Mark asked me what I thought of the idea. Characteristically, I neither encouraged nor discouraged him to accept the invitation. I did not agree to accompany him because of my concern that my visit would be interpreted as support for the Gaddafi regime. He did persuade Harold Romberg, a Regent from Spokane to accompany him. It was obvious that they had a great time. Later Mark discussed with me his desire to invite Gaddafi to visit the campus, and to give an address. This made me a little nervous, but again, I made no attempt to deny his right to do so. As I recall it, Gaddafi declined the invitation. In a way, I was disappointed for Mark's sake, but personally relieved. At the same time, I was given an opportunity to help Mark extend his understanding of an important international issue by not discouraging his trip to Libya nor by refusing to extend the invitation to Gaddafi to visit the campus.

James Schlesinger

Tom Pirie, Student Body President 1978-79, rounded up a group of students and marched to the president's residence to protest the speaking appearance of James Schlesinger, Secretary of Defense (1973) and Energy (1977). We were visiting on the deck at the president's residence, when Tom and a group of students came marching by, shouting in high-pitched voices their objections to our distinguished visitor. Neither Mr. Schlesinger nor I were offended by this mild demonstration. Even if we had been, we considered this an acceptable, if not the most genteel way for the group to make known their message. The interesting thing about this incident was the embarrassment of Tom. To this day, he has trouble being reminded of it. Tom is an excellent citizen, a highly valued school teacher, perhaps the most important public service one can perform. The experience provided Tom an opportunity to extend his education beyond the classroom through gaining additional information about an important opinion leader in American life at that time.

Apartheid

In the mid and late 1970s, there were huge pressures on universities to refrain from investing in companies doing business in South Africa, another opportunity to involve the campus in important social issues of the day. Again, a meeting with the regents was arranged for interested members of the university community, including students who were to make a presentation of their position on this important issue. The presentation was made, including the recommendation that WSU discontinue investing in companies doing business in South Africa. After much discussion, the regents adopted the Sullivan Principles, a set of conditions developed by a prominent African-American leader for universities to require of companies in South Africa in order to qualify for university investments. The Sullivan Principles centered on equality of treatment in such things as hiring, compensation, and work conditions.

Pac-10 Conference Membership

Paul Casey's political instincts and his successful first term as ASWSU President enabled him to become only the second student in history to be elected to a second term as president. During his second term, there was considerable discussion and disagreement among the students about the value of WSU's membership in the then Pac-8 Conference. Paul understood the academic importance of our being identified with the distinguished universities in the Pac-8 Conference: Washington, Oregon, Oregon State, Cal-Berkeley, Stanford, UCLA and USC and he was a big help in convincing other students of its importance.

Alcohol

During my tenure, dedicated, effective Student Affairs officers, including Art McCartan and Jack Clevenger and their associates, working closely with elected student leaders, dormitory and interfraternity Council officers and advisors assumed the responsibility for determining and administering rules on alcohol. The key to their effectiveness was the sense of responsibility the students felt about their leadership role, and what that role required of them. Of course, there were some violations of rules. But those who were violating rules were dealt with responsibly and often by the students themselves.

Much attention is being given today to this problem. It is universal. The stories of WSU being one of universities with the most serious problems caused by alcohol is a myth. I delegated the authority to staff officers and to student leaders. My experience lead me to believe that if the rules are sensible and student leaders are given much of the authority to determine and administer the rules, some violations will occur, but the magnitude of the problems will be minimal.

Stevens Hall

Here is another example of student involvement in important university decisions. The decision to preserve Stevens Hall, the oldest dormitory on campus, as a historical building was made only after students and former residents of Stevens had an opportunity to participate in the decision. I remember being a special guest at a reception at Stevens, and being treated like a savior. The students invited me to contribute a memento to the occasion. My gift was a cup, a family item that had been handed down to several Terrell generations. It gives me a warm feeling every time I think that future generations of Cougar women residents of Stevens have the cup. I know Catherine Friel was happy about the decision. She certainly influenced my "vote" as she frequently did.

Stimson Hall

When the business office of the university presented me with a proposal for replacing Stimson Hall with another structure, I gasped for air. I knew the men of Stimson loved their dwelling place, and would not give it up without a fight. I had learned that a leader should limit the number of issues she or he is willing to fight for. There is a limit to those that can be won, and I wondered if Stimson was one of them.

I arranged to meet with the men of Stimson, which, as I mentioned previously, was my custom. They turned out en masse. In fact, I believe that they imported some previous Stimson residents, or so it seemed. Anyway, we had a good conversation and I did most of the listening. I did not promise them anything except that I would ask the Vice-President for Business, Warren Bishop, to review the recommendation. He did, and the recommendation was changed. We would not, at least at that time, tear down their residence. This is merely another example of student involvement in non-academic decisions, important to students' personal development in terms of how to go about participating in change, a life-long involvement.

Students and the Vote

In the mid-1970s, student interest in the power of the ballot box became a much-discussed issue. This is important because of their concentration during that period on constructive approaches to bring about change, an aftermath of the more boisterous tactics of the unrest era. One of the most important outcomes, of this approach by the students, was the election of Bill Marler, an activist student (in the good sense of that term) to the Pullman City Council. Currently, Bill is a Regent at WSU and a successful attorney in Seattle, who specializes in defending the rights of citizens in malpractice suits. Paul Casey, along with Vice Presidents Mike Sweeney and Richard Slunaker deserve much credit for leadership in this era of very constructive student activity.

I cannot leave the student leaders chapter without mentioning the most important recognition I received at WSU, the conferring of the title, Honorary Student, by the Student Senate. Who has even heard of such an honor for a university president? Not me. As was the case with alumni, much of my work was centered on student leaders. As indicated for the alumni leaders, those student leaders who had the opportunity of being in office during the student unrest had the most difficult, but most interesting and challenging times to be a leader. They were Steve Kukuchi and Duncan Carter; Ray Crabbs and Dave Cardwell; Brian Benzel and Norm Davis; and Carlton Lewis and Scott Hendrickson. Also, the leaders during the eruption of the mountain in 1980, Gary Baker and Larry Clark, had an interesting experience.

All of the leaders in Table Four were very talented, and had the needed skills for the time they were in office. I consider all of them to be life-long friends. By this time, you will have noticed that student life permeates many of the experiences described in this book. That is no accident. My concept of a university starts and ends with an emphasis on students. I could never quite understand why some do not believe this to be the order of things. I am saving for a later chapter of the book, some incidents, vignettes, that occurred during my tenure that prompt me to smile, and remind me of one of the themes of this book. If a university president leads with the heart, she/he is likely to discover that followers follow with the heart.

Mt. St. Helens

To the best of my knowledge, WSU is the only major research university anywhere to be inundated with volcanic ash. The problems created by the explosion of Mt. St. Helens in May, 1980 created the strangest, and in many ways the most difficult campus upheaval of my time at WSU.

The mountain was spewing and "acting up" for several weeks before erupting. Seismologists predicted that an eruption was in the realm of possibility. On as beautiful a day as I have ever seen, at mid-afternoon it quickly became cloudy, and within an hour or so, Pullman was as dark as I have ever seen any night, anywhere. The news reports soon poured in over radio and television, informing us that the explosion had occurred. Surprisingly, western Washington had been spared except in the immediate vicinity of the mountain.

This ash cloud in eastern Washington should have been predicted because of the usual prevailing west-east wind pattern. The wind was pushing a voluminous amount of ash to central and eastern portions of the state. The ash fell for several hours. The telephones and doorbell at the president's residence rang angrily into the night, and the next day and night, a pattern that continued for about two weeks. Many students came to the "house" to see what I had to say about the bizarre events that were taking place. It became necessary to recruit student helpers to answer the phones and the doorbell. I must say, these students were exceedingly skillful, patient and mature in the way they handled the calls from alarmed and curious callers, parents and other students. Carolyn Rogers was especially helpful. I wish I could think of the names of the others. I definitely will never forget the help they gave me during a time when I truly needed them.

The next morning, I notified the campus that the university would be open, and that classes would be conducted as usual. I should have examined more carefully the condition of the sidewalks and streets before making that decision. The mistake was discovered immediately after I looked out the window and saw the clouds of ash that passing cars created, and when I personally inspected the difficulties that pedestrians including myself were having walking on the sidewalks. Within a few minutes, I sent out another notice that classes would be cancelled until further notice.

We obtained all the face masks that were available in the state, about three thousand, which was far less than we needed for everyone to have one. I made frequent visits to living units on campus, attempting to allay their fears. I don't remember having fear of the ash, and I don't know why. I think I was too busy to be afraid. Some students blamed me for the ash. After all, it occurred during my ministry. Some even yelled at me as I met them on my frequent walks on the campus after the explosion of Mt. St. Helens. They were my kids and I felt responsible for their health and welfare. One evening during a visit to Community Hall, one of the dorms, I encountered a group of about one hundred students. These students were angry and afraid and criticized me rather harshly, until they were lectured by another student, Lisa Gibb. One of them, upon seeing my face mask, angrily pointed out that I had a face mask, while she had only a bandana. I gave her my mask in exchange for her bandana. I don't remember ever wearing a mask after that until we had enough for every one on campus. I had the bandana the student gave me, and besides, the memory of the fact that I had a mask, when there were others in the university community who did not, still causes me pain.

About the only ecstatic people on campus were the geologists. They were in their element! How often would geologists associated with universities have a chance to increase their understanding of an important element of their discipline first hand? They were also very helpful to me and the rest of the university. I thank geology professor Ron Sorem especially for his assistance.

Our first need was to determine the composition of the ash. We appointed a group to advise us about that. Professor Leo Bustad, Dean of the College of Veterinary Medicine was leader of that group. He and the other scientists performed a great service to the university. They arranged to have the ash analyzed, which required four days. They determined that the concentration of granite, potentially the most harmful component of the ash was very low. So low, in fact, that it would require daily exposure to the ash on our campus for thirty years to create a risk of contracting the dreaded lung disease, silicosis.

This discovery created a tremendous relief from anxiety for the campus, until one day during our wait for the full report on the composition of the ash. The Daily Evergreen, the student newspaper, ran a misleading story accompanied by an electron microscopic photograph of the ash. The photograph revealed greatly enlarged, jagged pieces of glass with a caption something like, "The campus is swimming in a sea of glass." That's an example of the kind of *helpfulness* we occasionally got from student newspaper editors. And to think that early in my career, I recommended to the Editorial Board of The Daily Evergreen that we increase the number of issues from three to five per week. I point out that this was against the strong advice of Ray Crabbs, the President of the ASWSU. Ray has never let me forget that. But back to The Daily Evergreen report. To state that the news item once again stirred up the students is putting it mildly. We did learn that the report was accurate. There was indeed, glass in the ash. We also learned that the human organism is quite capable of neutralizing the glass by surrounding it with what is known as a microphage. News of this discovery helped settle the frayed nerves of the campus.

The next development consisted of a report, again in The Daily Evergreen, quoting a University of Washington geologist saying there was reason to believe that the ash was dangerous. The exact wording of the report escapes me, but I'll be generous and assume that they only wanted, as scholars, a complete review of the research literature on the composition of volcanic ash. Besides, why would scholars at our sister university in Seattle want to embarrass the State's "flagship" university in Pullman?

One other sideshow enveloped the campus during the aftermath of our exotic experience with the angry explosion of Mt. St. Helens. The sales of beer in Pullman surpassed all previous records! Keep in mind that students were asked to stay in their residences until we knew the composition of the ash. Apparently, the students, and maybe the faculty too, left their residences only to purchase more beer.

I have racked my brain in an attempt to invoke a general principle about university organizational theory that proved to be helpful to us in dealing with an obstreperous mountain! But I have failed to come up with anything. I warned you that some of the events would be managed by seat-of-the-pants judgment. This was one. I am reasonably confident that no library has documents pointing the way for the management of campuses inundated by volcanic ash. As mentioned earlier, it was the most difficult challenge, for a period of two or three weeks, that I had during my eighteen years. I have only one suggestion to make to my successors: Keep a supply of masks for everyone in the community — thirty thousand should do it — for the foreseeable future. Mt. Rainier is known to have exploded many years ago, and it will do so again. So will Mt. St. Helens. And the prevailing westerly winds will continue.

A Student's Perspective from Today

I thought this would be an appropriate point to reprint portions of a letter I received recently from a student-leader during my tenure at WSU.

"As with any leader, there will be detractors. I am sure that you would be the first to admit to hundreds of faults and dozens of mistakes made during your tenure. But this should not blind you, or your readers, to the important lessons that can be gained by reviewing your life's work in these pages.

"When tuition was increased by some amount, approaching $290 per semester (looking back, what a deal that was!), there were discussions between the undergraduate council on what students could do. Neil Opfer and Tom Hall invited several of us to a meeting to discuss a tuition strike. They proposed that we would withhold paying tuition, encourage hundreds of students to follow suit, the press would cover it and our concerns would find a voice. It was an admirable vision and the issue was worthy of public attention.

"They looked to me to carry the message. I had developed a reputation during the years of being a bit outspoken on the student council. I didn't spend much time studying, but I spent considerable time drinking coffee and getting to know other students. Neil and Tom realized that if I joined their effort, many more students would likely participate.

"As I lived on College Hill, I walked by the President's house almost every day, under those beautiful, large maple trees. The strike meeting was held in the evening, and I left the gathering uncommitted. I told I would think about it. The impact of the strike would be its public statement, not the volume of students who withheld their tuition. Ultimately, the university would make us all pay or leave, and I was unconvinced that we could organize more than a couple of hundred students to participate.

"It was after 9:00 pm, and as I passed the president's house, I noted that there was a light on in what appeared to be the office. I stopped for a moment along the street, thought about your outreach to the student council on your previous visit, and calculated that if you were not in your pajamas, you might be interested in talking this issue through with me.

"We sat in your office for over an hour, talking about the financial challenges of the university and the financial challenges of the students. We talked of the legislature, of the continuing need for increased funding for our important investment in our public university system and of options that were available. You immediately addressed the need for programs to protect the students who would have the greatest difficulty with a possible tuition increase.

"You kept referring back to how WSU was a community. Yes, it centered around students, but it also included the faculty, the staff, the town of Pullman, the alumni, the parents of students and the state. You used the term 'university,' but it was clear to me that you defined it in terms of the spheres that give this institution its sense of identity and reputation in the world. I had never considered the whole of the community before. I realized for the first time, that we as students at WSU were part of a larger identity.

"You talked of how actions taken can hurt the reputation of the university, and asked if other actions would be more effective. Then you made a statement that I heard several times during our many years of discussions together, 'I know, Mark, that you would never do anything to hurt the university.' You had emphasized throughout the last hour of discussion, that there was an environment of this campus, and a format, where one can ask the tough questions, and address the complex issues. But in the end, since we were part of the larger community at WSU, it required us to protect the reputation of the university by using the internal system of discussion that included a university president who would address the issue or concern. Based on our discussions, you committed to making student aid a higher priority as a result of the tuition increase.

"As I look back on my experiences with you at WSU, it is clear to me now how gifted you really are. You know that young people need reaffirmation, as they develop into adults. They need to be recognized when they get their obligations right. They need to be encouraged to carry their responsibilities for themselves whenever possible. They need to be reminded that they are part of the community-of-the-whole. As a result, they have an obligation to their community.

"You knew that the only way to help young people realize these realities was to show them respect: respect for their passion, respect for their intelligence and ideas, and respect for their desire to create a better world. All of this was combined with an expectation of greater service, and you did this with every student you knew by name, shared lunch with and opened your door to. At considerable cost to your family, you became a great man Dr. Terrell, an important teacher of the leaders of tomorrow; what I call, *a man of significance*. It is an honor to know you."

—*Mark L. Ufkes*
Associated Student Body President, 1977-1978

It is very important for me to thank the many colleagues who helped make the student experience at WSU both beneficial and enjoyable. Singled out for special attention are: Matt Carey, the Director of the Student Union, the center of the students' social life and many learning experiences; Lola Finch, Director of Financial Aid; Gus Kravas, Director of the Counseling Center; Stan Berry, Director of Admissions, and Jim Quann, Registrar. All of these colleagues provided excellent service for students and faculty members.

Chapter Seven

THE REGENTS

The regents have the ultimate responsibility for every aspect of the university. They and they alone have the authority to select and replace the president. In practice, they delegate much of their authority to the president, who in turn, delegates much of his/her authority to other officers, e.g. the vice-presidents, the deans and department chairs. The emphasis on delegation depends basically on the confidence the regents have in the president. The general understanding is that the regents determine broad policies, and the president administers those policies. But the regents define policies and executive functions, and sometimes change these definitions, particularly if they are losing confidence in the president. For obvious reasons, this is perhaps the most frequent source of conflict between presidents and their Boards. This was never a problem during my tenure.

The regents in the state of Washington are appointed by the governor. I was fortunate to have very effective regents appointed while I was at WSU. I mentioned earlier the excellent quality of the regents appointed by Governor Evans. Generally, the other governors also chose regents wisely. I can best support that statement by reporting that all regents at WSU without exception acted on issues that they believed were in the best interest of the university, not on political grounds. That, my friends, is miraculous. In all of my conversations with other presidents about their relationships with their regents, I don't recall anyone making such a claim. Our regents were all very successful people and took their responsibilities very seriously. They are the most sought-after appointments the governor makes. However, some did not seek the appointment. The State of Washington enjoys a history of regents who have refrained from involvement in what is typically considered administrative functions. This too is quite unusual.

In the State of Washington, regents receive only reimbursement for expenses incurred attending monthly meetings. As implied above, it is considered an honor to be a regent at all public universities, especially at WSU and the UW.

It is essential that a Board and the president have a good working relationship. That does not mean that they must agree on every issue that comes before them. But it does mean that they must find a way to work out any disagreements on what they both consider important issues. It never occurred to me that I would not be able to work with any of the regents, nor that I would not like them personally. In fact, I assumed that I would become a friend of each of them, which I did. The friendship with regents accounts for the fact that when I was in their hometowns, I often called them to suggest lunch or a get-together of some kind and they frequently invited me to their homes for dinner. The regents who served while I was at WSU were bright, decent, personable and successful. And most important, the depth of their commitment told me that their hearts were involved in contributing to the development of young people. The "heart and theory" theme of this book correctly reveals that I believe the heart, as I have defined it, "love, reflecting profound personal commitment," is the most important trait of the regents and the president. Integrity, vision, courage and energy are givens for the regents too.

University presidents are useless if the regents don't support them and for the most part approve her/his recommendations. For this to happen, it is necessary that the president spend as much time as is necessary to keep the regents informed about what is going on and what issues are to come before the Board. Perhaps the most important rule in the care of regents is to never surprise them.

Leaders come in all sizes, S-M-L (L to R) Lane Rawlins, myself and Sam Smith

An Editorial Cartoon by Shaw McCutcheon from the Spokesman Review: One of the funniest cartoons about a silly subject.

A young Mike Price,
Asst. & current Head
Football coach

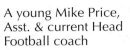

Jim Walden,
Head Football coach

Jim Sweeney,
Head Football coach

George Raveling, Head Basketball coach

BoBo Brayton, Head Baseball coach

Keith Lincoln 1982, Director of Alumni Relations

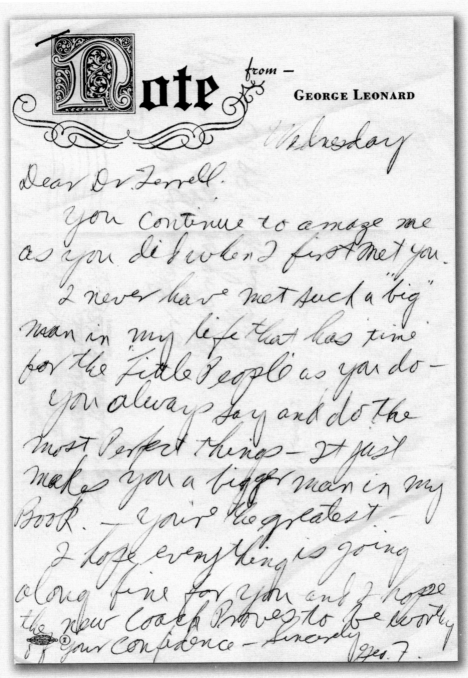

Letter from George Leonard, leader of Teamsters in Los Angeles, who persuaded Keith Lincoln to attend WSU.

Bob Smalley
and myself

Charles Smith,
Wallis Beasley,
James Conyers, and
James Short (behind)

Egyptian President Anwar Sadat, a great leader.

Board of Regents 1985. **Front Row** (L to R) Edie Williams, myself and Kate Webster. **Back Row** (L to R) Ed McWilliams, Dan Leary, Vit Ferruci, Jack Cole and "Charles" Chakravarti.

Mac Crow, one of my favorite Regents and friends. Boy, do I need a haircut!

Two of WSU's Regents with myself, Frances Owen and H. Dewayne Kreager.

A pleasant walk on Terrell Mall with Regents Bob McEachern and Kate Webster.

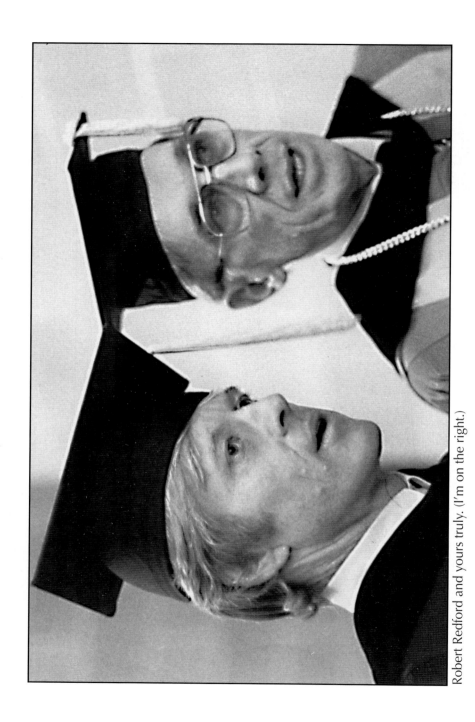

Robert Redford and yours truly. (I'm on the right.)

ASWSU President Reunion, 1980. Kneeling front (left to right): Connie Kravas (president, WSU Foundation), Brian Benzel, Mark Ufkes, Tom Glover; Standing (left to right): Roland Lewis, Paul Casey, Tom Pirie, John Winkler, Gary Baker, Rob Hoon, Chris Schlect

(L to R) Vann Snyder (ASWSU Assembly), Greg King (ASWSU VP), Mark Ufkes (ASWSU President) and Tom Pirie (Student Advisor of the City of Pullman) 1977

Larry Clark (ASWSU VP) and Gary Baker (ASWSU President) 1979-1980

Steve Kikuch,
ASWSU President 1967-68

Ray Crabbs,
ASWSU President 1968-69
with Rosalie Smith

Paul Casey,
ASWSU President 1973-74
and 1974-75

The Ministry of Leadership • 135

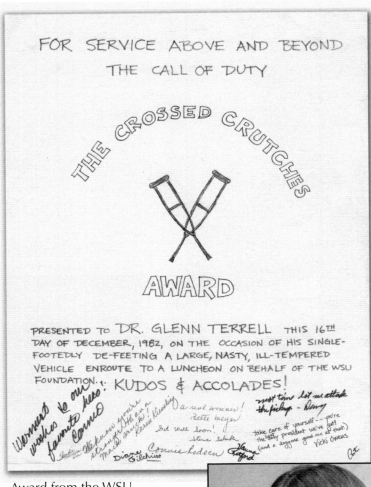

FOR SERVICE ABOVE AND BEYOND
THE CALL OF DUTY

THE CROSSED CRUTCHES

AWARD

PRESENTED TO DR. GLENN TERRELL THIS 16TH
DAY OF DECEMBER, 1982, ON THE OCCASION OF HIS SINGLE-
FOOTEDLY DE-FEETING A LARGE, NASTY, ILL-TEMPERED
VEHICLE ENROUTE TO A LUNCHEON ON BEHALF OF THE WSU
FOUNDATION.: KUDOS & ACCOLADES!

Award from the WSU
Foundation after I was hit by
a pick-up truck in Spokane.

Nola Cross,
Editor of The Daily Evergreen
and strong student leader
during campus activism.

Secret Intent, sired by Secretariat. A special race at Longacres after having been cured of Wobblers disease by members of WSU's Department of Veterinary Medicine.

Ken Alhadeff, current WSU Regent

(L to R) Tom Pirie, Terrell, Mark Ufkes, former ASWSU Presidents, who helped me with this book.

Lynn Claudon, consultant who helped me with the book.

Bill Vadino,
Alumnus who helped me
with the book.

Mikal Thomsen,
Alumnus and COO of Western
Wireless, also helped me with
the book.

Mike Bernard,
Alumnus and Seattle
attorney, who assisted
with the book.

Sue Hinz,
Provided extraordinary
research for this book.

Crimson Company entertaining at my retirement party.

Revealing my early opinion of retirement parties.

Chapter Eight

THE FACULTY

I remind the reader that my ultimate goal for WSU was to be admitted to the prestigious Association of American Universities in the not too distant future. The regents bought this vision, as did enough faculty, student and alumni leaders to make the vision feasible — one that would be reflected in necessary decisions to make it happen.

The faculty of WSU are the ones who made it possible for us to move toward a more distinguished research university. Our message to the governor and the legislature, as expressed in our budget presentations, included money to make this goal possible. Increased funds for salaries, equipment and the library were emphasized, but regrettably, usually only partially appropriated.

Four valid measures of the quality of a research faculty are the frequency of citations of their publications, memberships in honorary groups such as the National Academy of Sciences, their ability to attract research and training grants from outside sources, and leadership offices held in the appropriate disciplines. Table Five includes external funding during my tenure, 1967-1985 and for comparison, 2001.

Table Five
External Funding (Grants & Contracts) Grand Totals
Fiscal Years: 1967–1985; 2001

1967 8,897,113	1974 ...13,654,837	1981 37,879,924
1968 9,664,766	1975 ...15,740,013	1982 42,829,884
1969 9,279,845	1976 ...19,573,716	1983 46,342,253
1970 9,933,871	1977 ...19,636,655	1984 49,867,576
1971 ...10,313,863	1978 ...23,476,747	1985 42,678,566
1972 ...11,478,603	1979 ...26,898,315	2001...139,959,933
1973 ...12,181,511	1980 ...30,029,770	

The above amounts are provided by the WSU Institutional Research office. The figures reflected for 1967 to 1979 are disbursements. From 1980 to present, the amounts are based on incoming revenues. For our purposes, these distribution and revenue amounts will suffice.

As can be seen from the data in Table Five, there has been an overall increase of approximately $130 million between 1967 and 2001, more than a tenfold increase. Additionally, there has been approximately a fivefold increase between 1967 and 1985, and a threefold plus increase between 1985 and 2001.

The data from 1967 to 1980 are actual disbursements which the Office of Institutional Research reports are approximately the same as the grants and contracts for those years.

There were no faculty members in the National Academy of Sciences (NAS) in 1967. Since then, eight faculty members have been elected to this prestigious group. They are:

- R. James Cook, Plant Pathology (joined WSU 1965; elected to NAS 1993)
- Rodney B. Croteau, Institute of Biological Chemistry (joined WSU 1972; elected to NAS 1997)
- John P. Hirth, Applied Physical Sciences (joined WSU 1988; elected to NAS 1994)
- Linda L. Randall, Biochemistry (joined WSU 1981; elected to NAS 1997)
- Clarence A. Ryan, Plant Biology (joined WSU 1964; elected to NAS 1986)
- Diter von Wettstein, Plant Biology (joined WSU 1996;

elected to NAS 1981)

- John Slaughter, National Academy of Engineering (joined WSU 1979; elected to NAS 1982)
- Leo Bustad, National Institute of Medicine (joined WSU 1973)

I call attention to the fact that some of our Academy members are no longer with WSU. More often than not, faculty members leave our university to go to another position, too often because of WSU's inability to compete with counter offers in terms of salary, classroom and laboratory equipment, and library resources. The loss of excellent faculty members, and our failure to recruit those we very much wanted, caused me more grief than anything that happened while I was there, with the exception of the deaths of faculty, staff and students.

It gives me pleasure to give credit for the data regarding external funding and membership in the National Academy of Sciences with faculty and administrators of the Compton, Clement French and Sam Smith years. Furthermore, I am confident that the Lane Rawlins era will result in even more persuasive evidence of the high quality of our faculty members. Hopefully this will result in our becoming a member of the Association of American Universities during his tenure or soon thereafter.

The Intercollegiate School of Nursing

When I arrived on the campus in 1967, the clinical experience of WSU nursing students was in Spokane, which has excellent medical facilities, including several highly rated hospitals and clinics. In fact, Spokane is a medical center for parts of Washington, Idaho, and Oregon — the Inland Empire. Plans were being made to develop an Intercollegiate Nursing School. This plan became a reality several years later, when we were able to get a federal grant for a building to house the program. The cooperating universities are, in addition to WSU, Eastern Washington University, Gonzaga, and Whitworth. That program is serving the needs of the Inland Empire.

The federal grant was made possible through the efforts of

Senator Warren Magnuson and Congressman Tom Foley, yet another example of their interest and influence. I admire the competence and determination of the leaders in nursing education in the Spokane program, especially Hilda Roberts, Laura Dustin, Betty Anderson and their colleagues. They persevered even when the prospects of federal assistance did not seem too bright. It was a pleasure for me to work with such inspired colleagues.

Turf Wars: The Branch Campus Concept

The branch campus campaign was a drawn out affair, beginning before my tenure. I was hired as president of WSU to lead the future development of the campus in Pullman. At the same time, I recognized the need for programs in Spokane, the Tri-Cities and in the rapidly developing southwestern Washington area. It was obvious that the development of degree granting campuses in population areas of the state outside of Seattle was a political reality. Many other states had already gone through a similar expansion. My position was that whatever we did about that issue should be worked out with the cooperation of the independent colleges, particularly in Spokane.

At the same time, Eastern Washington University's expansive President, George Frederickson, was claiming in various ways that the Spokane area was Eastern's domain. He did wild sorts of things like buying buildings to house his planned expansion without the permission of the legislature. He also was engaging in an all-out effort to offer doctoral programs in Spokane that disturbed Gonzaga and Whitworth, as well as WSU. All of this despite the emphasis on cooperative efforts that were being made by the rest of eastern Washington's public and independent colleges and universities. I finally had enough of the lone ranger tactics employed by George, and proposed at a meeting of the House Appropriations Committee that Eastern Washington University become a branch campus of Washington State University. The rest of Frederickson's tenure was spent attempting to avoid becoming our branch campus. I got nothing but praise from the WSU faculty for that bold request. I didn't expect the legislature to approve my request, but it did make sense then and now, from an educational and, some would say, political sense.

The College of Veterinary Medicine

During the early years of my WSU experience, the College of Veterinary Medicine was not in good standing with the accrediting agency. The College, established at the turn of the century, was and always will be important to WSU. We recruited Leo Bustad to provide the leadership in restoring the College to its rightful place among America's premier Colleges of Veterinary Medicine. With the total cooperation of the faculty of the College, and the support of the Regents and the legislature, we soon removed the deficiencies. The College now is considered by those who know to be one of the nation's best Veterinary Colleges.

During the process of rebuilding the quality of the College, I became very interested in the profession of veterinary medicine. The developments that are taking place there are very exciting, and I am privileged to have been a part of them for eighteen years. In addition to Leo, I remember the contributions of faculty members like Barry Grant, Dick Ott, Jim Henson, Jack Alexander and Gherry Pettit, who co-authored the excellent history book on the College, and at another level, the unanimity expressed by the College on the replacement of Butch issue.

Another important development that took place during my tenure was the establishment of a Regional Veterinary Medicine Program. With the Universities of Idaho and Oregon this took place during an era of sharing resources for the development of expensive programs like veterinary medicine.

WSU also had an excellent program in large animal medicine. It included a specialty in the thoroughbred horse industry, with links to Morrie Alhadeff, the owner of Longacres race track in Seattle. Secretariat, generally conceded to be one of the best race horses ever, if not the best, sired a foal that had Wobblers disease. In the 1970s, this was a serious threat to the horse's racing career. Dr. Barry Grant, a professor in our college, led a team of colleagues who treated the animal, Secret Intent. Their treatment resulted in remarkable improvement, enough to cause Mr. Alhadeff's decision to hold a special day at Longacres to demonstrate the colt's improvement. With many fans present and cheering wildly, Secret Intent galloped majestically around the track and through the finish line in grand style. It was such a touching experience to those of us who admire horses, that I found myself with tears flowing down my cheeks. I looked at Morrie's face and he was teary-eyed also. I shall never forget that emotional moment! Morrie, very generously, gave half of that day's gate to each of Washington's two research universities, Washington State and Washington.

By the way, Morrie's son, Ken, is now an excellent regent of WSU. I remember how pleased I was that he attended my retirement party.

The WAMI Program (Washington, Alaska, Montana, Idaho)

Soon after I arrived in Pullman, the University of Washington, with a grant from the Commonwealth fund, established a cooperative medical school program with the states of Alaska, Idaho and Montana. At that time, the University of Washington was having difficulty producing enough doctors for the Northwest.

The WAMI plan was based on the assumption that the Universities of Alaska, Idaho and Washington state had the basic disciplines necessary to provide a sound program suitable for the first year of medical school. The University of Washington admits the medical students and then "farms" some out to Washington State, Idaho and Alaska for the first year, an ingenious plan that increases the number of MDs without the enormous cost of establishing another medical school in the region.

The medical students attending WSU in the program were frequently graduates of our pre-med program. I invited the WAMI students for dinner often, and found that they enjoyed the experience, especially because of the early contact with Pullman doctors and their patients.

Because of my early, strong support of WAMI, I was presented with a University of Washington Chair. I ask my many Cougar friends to forgive me. It would have been rude of me to have declined the gift.

The Faculty Survey

In 1980, I finally truly arrived as a successful, legitimate university president. Some of the faculty believed that I should bow out as president. The most frequently held reason, as I recall it, was the mistaken belief that I had allocated funds from the College of Engineering to intercollegiate athletics. What we had actually done was to skim several hundred thousand dollars for athletics off the total budget appropriated by the legislature, before the budget was allocated to any of the colleges and departments. This was known by the legislature and the Attorney General's Office, represented at that time by one of the most savvy lawyers I have ever known, Sally Savage. Positioned as we are in Pullman, there was no way at that time we could have maintained our membership in the Pac-10 Conference without help from the state.

There were undoubtedly other reasons that prompted the revolt of some of our faculty members. Earlier, I mentioned that, theoretically, the presidency is an impossible job. I'm sure that I displeased some people with many decisions I made. That's the nature of the position, especially for those of us who make decisions that we believe are consistent with the vision we have for the university.

A faculty group designed a simple questionnaire of two items, both of which requested a "yes" or "no" answer. The questions sought faculty opinion on whether or not the respondent was satisfied with the performance of the administration, that's me, and whether or not the president, that's me too, should be replaced. The approximate distribution of responses was as follows. Question One: two thirds "no"; one third "yes." Second question: 48 % "yes," 52% "no."

The faculty group appeared at a regents' meeting to report the results of the survey. Professor Jim Short, Director of the Social and Economic Science Research Center, assisted by Professor Don Dillman, one of the best survey research scientists, then made some comments about the lack of validity of the survey. Among other things, Dr. Short indicated that the distribution of ballots was inconsistent, some faculty members receiving no ballots, while others received several.

The regents then dismissed the faculty group making the report, the media folks and me, while they discussed the issue before them. The most vivid memory I have of this experience is how beastly hot it was out in the hall with my faculty colleagues and a bevy of members of the media with their bright lights, bulging eyes and question after question. One reporter from the Seattle Post Intelligencer came to my office after the meeting with additional questions, the main one being how I felt about a faculty survey that revealed many faculty members were not satisfied with the performance of the administration. I remember saying that if I had received a ballot (which I did not), I would have indicated dissatisfaction also, since it is my belief that I can always improve my performance in whatever I am doing.

The regents passed a resolution of support of the president, without a dissenting vote.

I have only two comments about this experience. I would have resigned if I had not been quite sure that I had the support of enough of the faculty members who were in essential agreement with the vision we shared for WSU.

The other comment relates to the Board of Regents' unanimity. Had they not been united, the efforts of the faculty group would probably have continued.

Chapter Nine
LEADERSHIP STYLE

The leadership style of a university president defines the way the president goes about the business of leading, and relating to members of the university community and numerous off-campus groups. There are no right or wrong styles. There are only effective or ineffective styles. Effective styles for one university may be ineffective for another. To complicate things further, an effective style at one stage in a university's development may be ineffective at another time at the same university. I served WSU when the events during my tenure, in some respects, demanded different styles and skills. The first few years demanded an ability to keep the peace: a respect for young people, patience, a willingness to listen, an ability to avoid taking criticism personally, and the refusal to allow the university to become politicized.

The next few years required an ability to "mend fences" with our off-campus constituents. There was much anger "out there" over the campus activism. I believed that my main responsibility was to defuse it and, for the most part, we did. However, meeting with these groups gave me an added perspective on public reactions to the way we had handled campus demonstrations. I still believe we handled the late 1960s, 1970 and 1971 wisely. But it was now the early and mid 1970s, and it was quite apparent that if we wanted to continue to have strong public support, some modifications needed to be made in the way we managed campus activism. These times required a somewhat greater firmness in our management of protests. When we explained this to campus groups, most seemed to understand.

Finally, the third period, the late 1970s through the mid-1980s was a time that demanded a different style, and a different set of skills. The continuing decline in public support, in terms of the percent of the State's General Fund appropriated for higher education, required the president and his associates to spend more time and energy fund raising with the legislature, alumni, corporations, and public and private foundations. The WSU Foundation, it will be remembered, was just getting started, but grew rapidly, simply because the faculty, alumni and corporate and foundation friends pitched in and immediately helped. I had a little difficulty at first, asking for money, but got over it when we raised a million dollars (a huge sum in those days) to replace the south stands of the football stadium. Among other things, I learned the importance of: 1) cultivation of prospective donors; 2) the appeal to the heart of the donor; and 3) that many prospects are waiting to be asked to contribute to WSU.

I will let history decide how well-suited my style and skills were to these three different time requirements. I would be surprised and actually somewhat disappointed if there aren't differences of opinion on all of these.

What about educational leadership? The role of the president has changed during the past several decades. Universities now place a greater emphasis in the recruitment of presidents with such things as political and fund-raising skills and the ability to relate to all kinds of constituents, on and off campus — the Regents, legislators, faculty, students and alumni.

There is still another reality that somewhat dilutes the role of the president in educational leadership — the concept of shared governance. The opinion of some of the faculty and students was that not enough authority was given to them in the important decisions. I confess to some degree they are right. Sometimes decisions have to be made without discussions with the faculty and students, as when I recommended to a legislative committee that Eastern Washington University become a branch campus of Washington State University. I received many supportive comments from both faculty and students. Sometimes I believe the faculty and students actually want the president to make decisions with a minimum of consultation or even no consultation, particularly when strong, assertive leadership is called for — especially when the university is under attack by off-campus individuals or groups. The insight and understanding of the faculty and students on the part of the president is crucial here. In other words, the president had better be correct in his/her judgment in decisions of this sort.

Still important, however, is vision for the future, and the ability to sell that vision to those who must support it. We were somewhat hampered in that regard during the period 1968-70, when much of our attention was directed toward keeping the peace on campus. Nevertheless, we stuck as closely as possible to our goal of greater emphasis on research and graduate education, while continuing the high priority of preserving the unique strengths in the undergraduate experience at WSU. I rarely missed an opportunity to make pronouncements about our priorities. Furthermore, budget decisions reflected our vision for the future. The role of the president in articulating that vision remains extraordinarily important.

In one of the most interesting and refreshing books on leadership I have read recently, Steven Sample, President of the University of Southern California, argues for what he calls a "contrarian's" style of leadership. Quoting Sample, "Conventional wisdom considers it a valuable skill to be able to make judgments as quickly as possible, and conventional wisdom may well be right when it comes to managers. But contrarian wisdom argues that, for leaders, judgments as to the truth or falsity of information or the merits of new ideas, should be arrived at as slowly and subtly as possible and in many cases not at all." Sample insists that leaders must learn to depart from binary thinking (seeing everything as black or white, right or wrong, etc.) and to learn how to, "Think gray and think free." He further explains that "thinking gray" is synonymous to the popular term "thinking out of the box," or "brainstorming." Thinking free "takes the process of inventiveness to the next level." Sample describes how one learns to think free by allowing your mind "to contemplate really outrageous ideas, and only subsequently apply the constraints of practicality, legality, cost, time and ethics."

I am describing Sample's contrarian leadership style in some detail, because it stresses the importance of cognitive skills in effective leadership. It also reinforces the research of Warren Bennis and others, who have found that leadership is not a function of size, gender, race or social class. Rather, effective leaders are distinguished from ineffective leaders in cognitive skills, or the way leaders think and encourage others to think.

Sample contends that learning to think free is anything but easy. He gives a hypothetical example of how the skill may be acquired as follows: An organization's top level executives meet to discuss how a particular company goal can be met. Everyone suggests an "off the wall" idea as to how the goal may be reached. Others are then asked to think of at least two reasons why the ideas presented WILL work. Sample reports that most people find it very difficult to force themselves to come up with reasons why some of these ideas have merit "for even a few minutes."

Another reason that Sample's style appeals to me is the success he has had in leading USC from a respected university to an outstanding one. I know of no better validation for his contrarian leadership style. He has made it work and he is still there. Applying his contrarian style to the question of whether or not it would have been effective at some previous period in USC's history, we can't say for sure. Would his contrarian style of leadership be effective in dealing with campus unrest or a volcanic explosion? I can certainly imagine that it is effective during a period of student calmness and in planning for educational development, when vision building and creativity are so important.

We have only discussed traits that characterize effective leaders. Are there stylistic traits that interfere with effective leadership? The answer is "yes." I have observed two related traits that appear to be inimical to successful leadership. Although I know of no research that supports my observation (which has never kept me from expressing my views), I have noticed that leaders who never seem to be able to consider the possibility that they bear the responsibility for having made a bad decision are not long in the job. It is refreshing for a leader to say, "I blew that one." It has a disarming effect on most followers, accept possibly on those who seek a pound of flesh. The other trait that tends to interfere with the effectiveness of leaders is the huge ego. A leader's confidence in his/her ability to lead (in Albert Bandura's term, a leader with high self-efficacy) is critically important. But a huge ego tends to be a trait of those who are uncertain about their ability to lead, and this uncertainty may show up as a strong need to be in control.

Much of this book about events that occurred and how they were handled reveal my own leadership style, especially in the preceding section. I'll be brief here. The best words to describe my style are *informal* and *accessible*. I did not want my assistants to "protect" me from anyone. The university, by definition, is owned by the people, and I wanted to know what the people wanted to tell me, whether it made me feel good or not. I wanted to behave in such a way that faculty, students, staff, regents, alumni, legislators and governors could detect my respect for them and their ideas, whether I agreed with them or not. Some were critical of my style, but like Steven Sample's style, it worked, for the most part.

Many people familiar with the history of presidential performance of the seven presidents who have served WSU tell me that all possessed the unique style and skill needed at the time of their selection. (There have been nine presidents in our history, but the first two were in office for such a short time there is not enough information for me to have a judgment about them.) If longevity in office is a valid basis for judging presidential performance, then one can reasonably agree with the claim that the regents have chosen wisely in each presidential appointment. Beginning with President Bryan, the average tenure of WSU's presidents is approximately fifteen years, about ten years longer than the average tenure. However, I don't think the ability to survive is a very good criterion for making a judgment about the quality of a president's performance.

The following descriptions of the presidents at WSU validate the commonly held belief that the regents choose wisely.

Former WSU Presidents

Brief sketches of the Presidents from Enoch Bryan through Clement French, including Interim President Wallis Beasley, appear below. I thank Gen DeVleming and Bob Smalley, two of the most knowledgeable associates about WSU history, for the excellent help they gave me in writing these sketches. These friends lived through the tenures of several former presidents. One could accurately say they helped "break us in."

Since I believe that President Bryan did more than any one of us so far in establishing the broad definition of WSU's role in Washington's higher education system, more attention will be given to his tenure than the others. His strong style and will were badly needed at the time he assumed office three years after WSU was established. Were it not for President Bryan's insistence and courage, we could very well be much more narrow in our program offerings than we are now. President Bryan understood the Morrill Act which created Land Grant Universities, calling for universities in all states to provide a broad experience in the Liberal Arts for those in Engineering, Agriculture, Veterinary Medicine, and Home Economics. We probably would be restricted in our offerings, particularly in doctoral programs in the Humanities and Social Sciences, were it not for President Bryan's efforts. His success in this role definition battle undoubtedly resulted in him being known as the "Father of the College."

Furthermore, Bryan is responsible for providing the groundwork for the fact that WSU was the first separate Land Grant university to have a chapter of Phi Beta Kappa. Understandably, in those days, the University of Washington opposed the broader role accorded WSU. In more recent years, the two research universities have had very good, mutually-beneficial, working relationships, especially in our work with the legislature. I think the record will show that Presidents French and Odegaard deserve credit as the first to begin a new era of improved relationships between the two research universities. This has continued to the present time by all presidents at both institutions. Understandably, there are some issues that divide us. An example of the latter is a change in the universities that WSU and UW compare themselves to for budget proposals to the governor and the legislature, particularly in determining the critically important faculty salaries. As long as this policy is in effect, faculty salaries at WSU will be lower than the UW, and by definition will be increasingly lower in the years ahead. Since this change took place during my watch, I must accept the blame, along with former governor Booth Gardner, the state budget officer and the members of the legislature who were in office at that time.

President Holland's tenure began in 1916 and continued for 29 years, the longest in WSU's history. There were many challenging events during these three decades: World Wars I, and II, conflicts with the University of Washington, and a student demonstration over what the students considered to be unreasonable rules governing appropriate behavior for both men and women.

In 1927, the first chapter of Phi Beta Kappa at any separate Land Grant University in the nation was established. Soon after President Holland became president, the college was divided into five colleges and four schools, including the Graduate School. Earlier in 1922, the radio station began operations. Very significantly, in 1939 the Board of Regents approved President Holland's recommendation for the establishment of the first retirement system. The events of the Holland years support the belief that he was the right person for his time. The library was named for President Holland.

President Compton, for whom the student union building was named, took office in 1945, just as the huge enrollments following the end of World War II descended upon the campuses. This necessitated large increases in physical facilities, as well as faculty and staff. Todd, Johnson and the library were built. Compton convinced the Board that a reorganization of research and extension was needed, as were changes in the organization of Athletics and other components of the university. Quick changes were made in other programs.

The acquisition of property at the upper end of Priest Lake was a significant change, especially for those who acquired some of the beautiful sites for vacation homes.

Rapid changes always place a strain on many components in an organization. WSU was not immune to some of the disruptions that change creates. It is my impression that most of the changes initiated during President Compton's tenure were badly needed.

William Pearl served as Interim President in the academic year, 1951-52. An interim president's job is to provide continuity and stability from the president's office and the rest of the university. From all reports, he did an excellent job doing just that.

Clement French became president of WSU in 1952. The most important event during his administration was the decision to change the name of Washington State College to Washington State University. After all, we had been producing Ph.D.'s for many years, one of the criteria for the University title. President French was a fine gentleman. I enjoyed many conversations with him in the building which bears his name, where he also had an office. He was available for advice and discussions on any topic, but it was quite obvious that he was happy to pass on the heavy responsibilities to his successor. Only those who have served as a university president can fully understand why.

Other important contributions President French made are the establishment of the Faculty Invited Address, the Honors Program, the university television station (KWSU) and the Regents Distinguished Alumnus Award. President French had a keen sense of humor, a very valuable trait for a president. He liked to tell you that he arrived as president on April Fool's Day and left on Halloween.

Wallis Beasley was Interim President of WSU during the academic year 1966-67. The Regents could not have selected a better person to provide continuity. In fact, Wallis would have been an excellent president of WSU or elsewhere. We were fortunate to have his loyal and strong leadership capabilities for several decades in many important positions, including Chair, Department of Sociology, Academic Vice President and Executive Vice President.

Based on these brief sketches, it is clear that the presidents selected possessed the skills needed at the time of their selection.

Chapter Ten
INTERNATIONAL PROGRAMS

O ver the years, WSU has had several international programs, sponsored by the U.S. State Department's Agency for International Development. One with Pakistan was nearing completion when I arrived. Four programs were undertaken and completed while I was president: Jordan, China, Egypt and Indonesia. Still other programs of student and faculty exchange were arranged by our International Office, mostly in Western European nations, but also included Taiwan and China.

When I arrived at WSU, the program in Pakistan established during President French's years was near completion. Another one in Jordan was in the works. I made one trip to Jordan, a program concentrating on the development of a College of Agriculture. The main purpose of my trip to Jordan was ceremonial in nature, but important, nonetheless. My impression was that we served the needs of Jordan in an excellent manner.

WSU, along with the University of Missouri, working with Egyptians based in Washington, DC, developed a program designed as a follow-up to the Camp David Accords. Our plan was to explore with our Egyptian friends the various possibilities that existed for our nations for cooperative, economic, cultural and educational development programs. The University of Missouri's President, accompanied by several associates, and myself, made two trips to plan the meeting. Congressman Tom Foley led our party to Egypt to participate jointly in the seminar with the Egyptian counterparts. Tom did his usual excellent job representing the United States. The seminar, held in a hotel in Alexandria on the Mediterranean Sea, was an excellent example of how two friendly nations can cooperate on a program jointly designed. Unfortunately, the amount of actual follow-up was limited by the assassination of Egypt's superb leader, Anwar Sadat.

On one of our planning trips to Egypt, our party visited many sites of great historical and symbolic importance, including the pyramids, the museum, and a dinner on a boat on the Nile River, complete with excellent food and entertainment by belly dancers. Despite the charm and athleticism of the dancers, the highlight of our planning visit was an opportunity to visit with a man whom I believed to be the world's greatest leader at that time, Anwar Sadat. We spent an extraordinarily interesting hour with him at his home, followed by an equally outstanding hour with his wife. We were and are grateful to our Egyptian friends for arranging these meetings.

In the late 1970s, I went to Indonesia, sponsored by the Asia Foundation, to explore the possibilities of a sabbatical in that country. I had been in the office of the presidency at WSU for ten years, and felt the need to spend some time overseas, in one of the so-called "developing" countries where I might be of some value. Earlier trips to Taiwan and Thailand sparked an interest in that part of the world. In fact, I was exploring the possibility of a sabbatical in Thailand, when the trip to Indonesia materialized. It turned out to be a beneficial and interesting experience.

Indonesia's population is the fifth largest in the world. From the easternmost island to the westernmost, it is about the same distance as from the eastern seaboard to the west coast of the United States. Jakarta, the capital and the main population center, is in the eastern part of the nation. The Asia Foundation was interested in assisting the government to develop higher education institutions in several eastern Indonesian islands. I was there to explore my interest in working in those developments for six to twelve months while on a sabbatical leave from WSU. The challenges of such an effort were great. The colleges in eastern Indonesia were not far along in their development, but the government in Jakarta was obviously committed to their further development.

My interest in assisting the Indonesian government was strong. But I could see the immediate need was not for one person on a sabbatical leave, but for the involvement of an entire university for several years. Accordingly, WSU applied for a multimillion dollar grant from the Agency for International Development (AID) for the project. AID officials in Washington, DC approved a seven million dollar grant to us for a multi-year period, and we went to work implementing the plan. For obvious reasons, many of the AID grants were primarily for the development of agriculture. But the Indonesia grant included other academic and staff departments, as well as faculty and student exchanges.

There were several exchange students on the Pullman campus for many years. They were an interesting, conscientious group, and seemed to enjoy being a part of the WSU life. We sent interested faculty and staff members to Indonesia, most of whom enjoyed the experience in that interesting part of the world. Of the many things that happened while our Indonesian friends were visiting was the explosion of Mt. St. Helens. They were delayed a day or two arriving in Pullman. They thought our excitement and fear of the ash was "much ado about very little." Indonesia is in the "ring of fire," those nations most likely to experience volcanic eruptions. They considered Mt. St. Helens a tame eruption compared to those they experienced much more frequently.

In 1982, Governor Spellman headed a party to mainland China to establish a friendship relationship between the State of Washington and the Sichuan Province. The Governor's party included about 25 political, business, agricultural and education leaders. President Gerberding of the University of Washington, and I were included in the party.

Our first stop was Beijing. We visited the Great Wall, Tiananmen

Square, the museum and other historical places before proceeding to Chengdu, the capital of Sichuan Province. There Governor Spellman did the honors for our group, required in the ritual celebrating the establishment of our Province-State relationship. This was an impressive occasion created by our friends, the leaders of the province. The formal dinner was a superb fifteen course affair, accompanied by many friendly "cheers," or "bottoms up." We did our best to keep up with our Chinese friends. Not to have done so would have been considered rude.

President Gerberding and I established relationships with several colleges and universities in Chengdu and Chongqing, the noodle capital and Seattle's Sister City. The relationships led to faculty exchanges, which were still active the last time I heard about them. I maintained contact with two of our Chinese colleagues for many years. It was an interesting experience. We did some shopping while we were in Chengdu. In 1982 the people were very curious about Americans. They followed us on the streets and in the stores, with curious expressions on their faces. Not once did I detect anything at all except curiosity and friendliness. Our last stop was in Shanghai, which even then was more westernized than any city we visited. I felt as if we had almost returned to the United States.

Chapter Eleven
RETIREMENT

The most important thing about retirement is that the person retiring has the good fortune and sense of timing in setting his/her own retirement date. For this reason, I informed the regents several years before my sixty-fifth birthday that I would not stay beyond age sixty-five. I regard it as nothing short of a miracle that I was able to survive so many events, any one of which could have caused me to retire or be retired. First was the peace-keeping role during campus unrest triggered by the Vietnam War and racism. Then came the need to win back our supporters who were in varying degrees alienated by excesses on the campuses. Finally was the fight for financial survival.

I feel it important to attempt to explain why I think I was able to survive three difficult periods with some effectiveness. As explained previously, my heart's devotion (my profound personal commitment) to the idea of a university and to the WSU community specifically gave me mental and physical strength to meet the three quite different demands of the times discussed above. Certainly my fondness and respect for students was a huge factor in managing the campus turmoil. My ability to mend fences and my willingness to accept criticism helped me through the difficulties in reestablishing rapport with our off-campus constituents following campus activism. My steadfast refusal to interpret criticism as a personal attack, either on or off campus, helped immensely.

The money problems of the 1970s and 1980s presented in some respects the most difficult era. First we established the WSU Foundation. The data referred to in the chapter on the Foundation has been a big factor in addressing the fact that state appropriations expressed as a percent of the State General Fund have gone down for the past thirty years. How can one avoid predicting a continuing reduction of state funding, again expressed in terms of the percent of General Fund allocations for public higher education, and a concomitant increase coming from student tuition and fees, and gifts and grants through the WSU Foundation? With this trend will come a continuing movement away from our long-standing commitment to the democratization of higher education in our nation, and a movement toward higher education only for those who can afford to pay. In other words, education strictly for the elite, like it was in earlier times.

Retirement parties seemed quite unnecessary, even boring, where the truth was often stretched in compliments about the retiree. However, attending the two retirement parties, one in Pullman and the other Seattle, gave me an entirely different perspective on the purpose and value of these time-honored events. One is to give recognition to the outgoing president. The other, more important purpose is the opportunity it provides for the alumni, faculty, students and state officials to get together in large numbers to rally around the "Cougar flag" in a show of force. For the Seattle party, it was "take over" Seattle for a day at the largest hotel with the largest banquet room in the city the center of "Huskyism." Accordingly, my support for the presidential retirement party is strong.

Another noteworthy incident that I remember occurred during the last year of my presidency — the routine action taken by the Board of Regents to evaluate my performance and to make any change in my salary they thought was appropriate. For the last five months of my tenure they approved an increase in my annual salary from approximately $90,000 to $104,000. The paperwork for this action was on the desk of my assistant, Gen DeVleming. While Gen's attention was briefly diverted, the editor of the student newspaper, who was in Gen's office, saw the paperwork on the regents' action on my salary on Gen's desk. He wrote a story in the student newspaper about this information, which did not take long to spread to other newspapers in the state. There was a barrage of criticism throughout the state, including some from members of the legislature. The adverse opinion was based on the amount of the increase, and the fact that the action was taken in a closed meeting of the regents.

Apparently there were many critics who did not know that personnel decisions in closed meetings were legal. I discovered that some people, even some legislators, thought that I had engineered that decision. I never spoke with any of the regents about my compensation. That was their job, not mine. In fact, decades earlier I complained about my salary increase once when I was a young assistant professor. That experience embarrassed me so much that I promised myself I would not ever do it again. I was true to my promise. I must have known, even then, that teaching, research and ministering to the needs of young people had far more to do with the heart and serving others than monetary reward.

Because of the uproar, I asked the regents to rescind the action and add it to my successor's compensation, as that much and more would be needed to get a first-rate president. The regents, with one exception, approved my suggestion. I also believed that my effectiveness in Olympia in my final budget presentation would have been adversely affected had the action of the Regents not been rescinded. I did appreciate the fact that the Regents thought that my performance was worthy of the increase.

My reaction to the whole issue was one of embarrassment. Not embarrassment for me, but embarrassment for the people who were so upset because they could be so out of touch about the market compensation for major university presidents. The good news is that it is all a thing of the past. I doubt anyone even remembers it, and if they do, they may be like me now — amused at the aggressiveness of the student editor, and how excited he must have been when he discovered he had scooped such "earth-shaking" news.

One final note about the retirement process in universities. In my opinion, the ancient custom of the retiring president giving a year's notice of the impending retirement is sometimes wise and sometimes unwise. In many instances, there is a qualified person currently in the university who can provide competent leadership while the search for a continuing president is being conducted. That custom must have been initiated by an egocentric president who thought it would take at least a year to find a successor of his/her caliber. The lame duck phenomenon applies in either case, but probably more so in the case of a retiring president than an interim president. In my instance, I did not feel nor act like a lame duck, but others did. It's only natural to do so. There is another reason for my opinion on this subject. Once the decision is made to retire, the departing person understandably tends to concentrate on the life or opportunity ahead rather than the position she/he is leaving.

Chapter Twelve
IN CONCLUSION

The previous chapters contain experiences related to goals, themes, and accomplishments at WSU during my tenure. I have attempted to apply my concept of university leadership, explicit in the title of this book, with the emphasis on heart, (profound personal commitment), ministry (service to others and the organization) and theory. Tests of this "theory" have been presented through data showing the improvement of our university in several ways:

- Improved scholarly performance and recognition of the faculty
- Increasing demand for the admission of undergraduate students who continue to value their WSU experience
- Strengthened ability to attract needed funds through the formal creation of the WSU Foundation
- The management of WSU during critical periods of emotional upheaval was sound (Nobody was killed or, to my knowledge, even injured.)
- Progress was made in university governance including the establishment of the University Senate with student membership
- I was included among fourteen university Presidents invited to the Wingspread Conference who were successful in their management of the student activism period

I commend my predecessors, Presidents Bryan, Holland, Compton, French, and Interim President Beasley, for the excellent work they did in establishing a pattern of stability and sound management at WSU that made my job much easier.

I hope that this book addresses the issues that the Wingspread Conference intended and that it proves to be helpful to future generations of university presidents and governing boards. It is one person's report on what principles of university leadership he found to be necessary. I have repeated these principles several time because of my exceedingly strong belief in their importance to me. Heart and Ministry may sound like old fashioned notions. I admit to having some old-fashioned ideas about some things. But I am not aware of research that rules out the effectiveness of profound personal commitment and a desire to provide human service as important traits for successful university leaders.

I have stressed the importance of the president having a theory, along with a set of assumptions, about the purposes and functions a university performs for society. It is this theory, as it relates to the institutional goals and priorities, that gives meaning to the many decisions the president makes.

One final point. It is not enough for the president to have profound personal commitment and a desire to serve others. Her/his close associates must be driven by the same commitments and goals. My associates were. Their good work and spirit were essential for every worthwhile goal we accomplished.

The eighteen years I was at WSU were demanding, yes, but challenging, memorable and exciting. I never wanted to leave WSU for another university, as many university presidents do, and as Paul Castleberry said to me, there were many challenges remaining at WSU. I shall never forget those challenges, no matter how long I live. I was privileged to have had the opportunity to serve WSU, and in retrospect, have good feelings about all of my colleagues there (some better than others, of course, but all good): regents, students, faculty, alumni, staff and the people of our State. My thanks to all who made it possible for me to serve you during several critical times during WSU's history.

Chapter Thirteen

VIGNETTES AND MEMORIES

N ow for the vignettes, the true stories that enriched my life as WSU's president. No chapter is more important than this one. Each story tells me directly or indirectly that we did some things right. These stories are in no particular order. The incidents and people involved are as fresh in my memory as if those eighteen years were only yesterday.

Presidents must have fun. Many little things in university life, even the big issues, can bring happiness. The ability to see the humor even in serious things, while doing one's best to take care of responsibilities, helped me to have a more balanced perspective of the problems at hand. I had difficulties refraining from laughing at a few of the demonstrating students. For example, when 3000 students "visited" me one evening at the president's house in the spring of 1970, there was not room for all of them in the front driveway, the street, as far as one could see up the hill and down the hill, and across the street in the neighbors' yards. Consequently, 20 or so students were perched in the trees in the front yard of the president's house, yelling epithets at me.

༄༅

I have one incident to tell that had a definite effect on my decision to accept the offer to come to WSU. Regent Kreager called me at my home in Arlington Heights, Illinois to urge me to accept the offer to become the president at WSU. He wanted to be sure that I knew that the Regents and others involved in the decision were unanimous and very strong in their desire to have me become their president. That meant much to me. I did not want to accept an offer on a split vote.

❧

Another incident involved a student who called me in a very angry state of mind because her dormitory did not serve lunch the last day before a vacation. I listened in my usual patient manner, then told her that I would make her a peanut butter and jam sandwich, and that she could pick it up at the president's house at noon. Of course, she expressed surprise at my response, but not so surprised that she failed to pick up the sandwich. I wonder how many other people she has told of this experience.

Incidentally, either June Gillette, Edris Bontadelli or I made the peanut butter, the bread and the jam, most likely by June or Mrs. B, the housekeepers and hostesses during most of my time at WSU. Both of these women were loyal Cougars, and did a great job taking care of the countless visitors at the "big house." They became part of the family. They have both retired. June still lives in Pullman and Mrs. B, now in her nineties, lives in Moscow. June continues to keep in contact with many students, past and present. She also continues to bring me raspberries from her own patch. The other assistant at the big house was, and still is, Bea Taylor, the housekeeper. She, like June and Mrs. B made herself indispensable. Always cheerful and upbeat, Bea, a saucy soul, like June and Mrs. B loved students. Among all of the good traits these women possessed, the one most important to me was their love of students.

❧

I became acquainted with many parents of students. Often I called them when I was in their home town, either to tell them something about their sons or daughters that I had recently learned, or merely to keep in touch. It was my way of telling them that we had a personal interest in them and their children. I wish it had been possible for me to express that concern to all of the parents of our students. It seems so simple, and yet so true that there is absolutely nothing in the universe that will please a parent as much as knowing that their sons and daughters are well and happy, and being well cared for. That is an important part of the ministry of higher education.

Those who sent me email messages, urging me to write the book, often mentioned the importance of my friendly and encouraging comments in my conversations with them on the campus. That seemed to add to their enjoyment of being a student at WSU, that they were not just a number.

One of the saddest experiences I had with the parents of one of our students occurred in the late 1970s. Student Kim Hanby contracted a serious disease which required many operations, which, over a period of time, robbed her of energy, but never the will to live. She was an inspiration to me. I visited her frequently at the hospital in Seattle when business of the university required me to be in town. She and her close friend, another student, Mary Tormey from Spokane, had been most supportive of me at a difficult time, and I had great fondness for both of them. Kim had profound inner strength and resiliency, but finally, much later than most so afflicted, she succumbed to the dreadful disease.

I kept in close touch with Mr. and Mrs. Hanby for many years. Relating this experience is a reminder that it is time to check in with them to see how they are. Also I want to add that my association with Mary Tormey and her family was one of the most enjoyable of my experiences at WSU. Mary's sister, Julie, and her bother Bill also attended WSU, while her other siblings, Janie and Peter had the misfortune of attending the UW and Chris the University of Idaho. I had the good fortune of visiting the family in their home in Spokane, which was always great fun. Bill and Margie Tormey, the mother and father, like all of the siblings, were very

friendly and outgoing. Bill always gave me a bear hug, which sometimes caused me to wonder if I had any broken ribs.

⊂≥⊱

Recently, I heard that a former WSU student Dan Harmon
had created a student scholarship endowment at WSU in
Vancouver in my name. The reason for his doing this occurred
many years ago at Pullman. One of his professors had told Dan
that he would not recommend him for admission to law school
because he had elected to take the grade he had just before the
final examination (an option we permitted as a consequence of
the disruptions that occurred on campus during the late spring).
As a last resort, he talked to me about this, and I promised to get
back in touch with him after I checked into the problem. Of course,
I made no attempt to call his instructor. (I have no idea who his
instructor was.) I did discover that Dan was a good student. I then
told him that I would be glad to recommend him to law school
on the basis of his general academic record, which I did. Many
years later, he gave WSU a major gift. He had not forgotten that I
helped him. He has since added to the endowment. Significantly,
he declined my suggestion that the endowment be in his name
instead of mine.

⊂≥⊱

Alan Barnsley, a professor of English, owned a 1951 Bentley.
He had brought it with him from the U.K. when he came to WSU.
Eventually, he quit driving it. 1951 Bentley's had no power steer-
ing and power breaks only on the rear wheels. I had seen Alan
driving it on campus occasionally for several years, and admired
its classic lines and general appearance. Then I realized that I had
not seen the Bentley for some time. Alan and his wife came to the
president's house for a reception, which gave me an opportunity
to talk to him about my concern at not having seen his elegant
automobile for a long time. That's when I learned that it was un-
licensed and resting on blocks in his garage.

I told Alan that if he would like to sell it at any time, I would
like to talk to him about buying it. I spoke to him in a very gentle

manner, out of consideration of him and that regal automobile. To my surprise, before he left the reception, he said he would like to sell it to me. Out of consideration for the Bentley, we agreed on a price without any haggling, just what it cost Alan, $2500. Those were the days before academic people became entrepreneurs. From that day on, my standing with students, faculty and staff zoomed at least until it came tumbling down because of a decision of some sort. Many colleagues, particularly students, loved that elegant carriage. In fact, many students would ask me how the Bentley was, often forgetting to inquire about me. While I am on the Bentley subject, I want to thank Steve Duncan for the excellent care he gave the Bentley. Steve's affection for this noble car led him to make a replica of it in mahogany which is in a very noticeable place in my study. He is as talented as a wood carver as he is in caring for a beautiful automobile. He loved that car as much as the students and I did.

Joan Collins, a former WSU student, and her mother and father from Spokane, became very good friends. Joan is a very talented young woman who has made a name for herself in Los Angeles in computer graphics and related fields. She used her talents in developing some of the programs for the Olympic games in Los Angeles several years ago. She sent me recognition items she was awarded for the quality and originality of her work. I was touched by her desire for me to have those items, which are now in a conspicuous place in my study.

Barbie Bangs the daughter of Benton Bangs Jr., and the granddaughter of Benton Bangs, Sr., — the football player on the 1916 Rose Bowl team — also graduated from WSU while I was there. Barbie, always thinking of others, arranged a birthday party for me, which included a special viewing of the planetary system at the university. "Charles" Chakravarti, one of our Regents at the time was also included in the party. Barbie, leaving no stones unturned in her plans for the event, included a limousine ride from the president's residence to the campus. It was a delightful evening, thanks to Barbie and Dan Diamond, another alumnus who jointly planned this special event. Incidentally, Barbie is a lawyer in the Bay Area in California, and Dan is an M.D. in the Puget Sound area. On another occasion, Dan also arranged a dinner at the president's house for a group of students. I had told Dan that I would be the waiter, at least for the first course. When I came out of the kitchen to the deck with my apron, the students did a double take. As I remember it, June Gillette provided a professional touch for the rest of the dinner, while I joined the students. Events like this are never forgotten by students, nor by me.

◈

Don Larson, an alumnus from Yakima, came to the campus often, especially to football games. He never failed to bring fruit with him. He was a colorful person in many ways. He always brought a container that had an innocent appearance, as if the contents were coffee or chocolate milk.

◈

Phil and June Lighty, the most devoted and generous alumni, often invited me to their ranch house in Kilroy, California. It was a treat to be in their home. There were plenty of laughs and a few serious conversations, mostly about WSU and the very productive fig tree that one of his friends had. Phil had been given permission to help himself to figs whenever he wanted some of those delicious treats. He did, and I got in on one of those visits. I've never seen so many figs consumed by anyone before or since then.

◈

I remember the hunting and fishing expeditions with Jim Henson, professor in the College of Veterinary Medicine. Jim was the best hunter and fisherman I have ever known. That covers a lot of territory from a person who was brought up in the southeastern part of the United States, and also loves the out-of-doors. He also is the best dog trainer I've ever known. His English pointers were superbly trained. I was not that bad, myself, having been in the business during my adolescent years of breeding and training bird dogs, pointers and setters. We hunted quail and chukars on the breaks of the Snake River, near Clarkston, Washington. And I can assure members of animal rights groups, and I am now one of them, that I was never a threat to those beautiful, exotic creatures. But the change of pace did wonders for my well-being. I thank Jim for that.

Two years after I retired, I moved to Seattle for several reasons, one of which was to be closer to my two children, Francie and Glenn, who were adults then, but age nine and twelve when we moved to Pullman. Also, I had been offered a position with The Pacific Institute in Seattle. And besides, retired university presidents are suppose to disappear. I found an opportunity to continue an interesting, productive life away from the constant pressures of the presidency. I also found that in Seattle, my life continues to be enriched by my friends, the former students from WSU. Some of my happiest experiences are chance meetings with Cougars in restaurants, hotels, meetings, receptions, on buses and the sidewalks in Seattle. One day, the first three people I saw when leaving my office were three former WSU students. We could have had a mini-alumni meeting right there. It was obvious that greeting each other brought a special warmth to all of us. I was a symbol of their fondness for their university. It is a priceless feeling that I can provide that symbol.

One day recently, as I was leaving my office, I got in my car to meet a friend at a restaurant. The alarm system was making an awful noise that I could not fix. Since I was already late for my appointment, I started off with the alarm still screeching. I had not gone more that a block or two, when a State Patrol car flashed me to a stop, and an officer approached my car carefully. I rolled the window down, and she asked me in a hesitant manner, "Is this your car?" When she looked at my driver's license, she remembered me from her WSU days. After a brief visit, she succeeded in stopping the alarm, and then asked me to drive carefully.

Two other times while I was at WSU, I was stopped by a State Patrol car. Once, between Pullman and Spokane, by an officer who forgave me with a lecture, and on another occasion between Seattle and Olympia, by an officer who wasn't so willing to excuse me with a nice lecture. That experience cost me about fifty dollars, as I remember. This officer was entirely unimpressed with the fact that I was in a hurry to get to Olympia to attend a meeting with the governor. I was very proud of the fact, and I told him so, that I was traveling only sixty five miles per hour. I had heard that as long as one doesn't exceed the limit by more than five miles per hour, the Patrol would not intercede. He responded unemotionally that the speed limit was sixty miles per hour. I was late for the meeting, but, as is often the case, I did not miss anything except the fifty dollar fine.

❦

Soon after arriving in Pullman, one of our Regents, Dutch Hayner, invited me to go huckleberry picking in the Priest Lake area. I had never been huckleberry picking before, and the idea struck me as being fun. It was, for the most part. Little did I know that an innocent berry-picking outing was about to present a test in how not to cultivate good relations with Regents.

We found out the huckleberries were in short supply due to the fact that the bears had been there first. And bears don't leave anything in berry patches but stripped stems — no berries, no leaves, no nothing. After what seemed like many hours (it was probably only an hour), the two of us had less than a quart, with Dutch having quite a lot more than I had. Dutch, attempting to cross a shallow ravine over a fallen tree, fell headlong in the dense underbrush. My instant reaction was concern that the berries he had were scattered over a large area that would require forever to retrieve.

Impulsively, I dashed over to where one of my bosses lay in the ravine, stunned by the fall, and yelled, "Did you spill the berries?" Minutes later, after partially recovering some of my composure and disappointment, I asked, "Are you O.K.?" After discovering that he was indeed OK a sinking feeling gripped me. What will he think of me? What will Jeannette, his wife think of me? What will the other Regents think? Luckily, Dutch has a great sense of humor, and I discovered that he even enjoyed telling others about the experience.

❧

Several times a year, I have lunch with former student leaders just to catch up on what's going on in our lives. Those usually attending are Mark Ufkes, Paul Casey, Mike Bernard, Mike Morgan, Mikal Thomsen, Lynn Claudon, Mark Elliot, Bill Vadino, Glenn Osterhout, and occasionally Mike Cohen. These get-togethers are open to those who wish to attend. Mark Ufkes is the one who usually gets us together. These meetings are thoroughly enjoyable. There is no agenda. We mostly talk about WSU.

One of the things this group planned and executed was my eightieth birthday party a couple of years ago. As I understand it, tireless Mark Ufkes lead the way on this event, but he was ably and enthusiastically assisted by others in the group and by the Alumni Association and the WSU Foundation, in both Pullman and Seattle. Mikal Thomsen graciously provided wine. It was a great party which included about a hundred celebrators: alumni; my family, Gail, my children and grandchildren; several former regents; several associates from The Pacific Institute, including Lou and Diane Tice and Jack and Judy Fitterer; the current ASWSU President, Steve Wymer; former athletic directors Ray Nagel and Sam Jankovich; and last but far from least, the new, at that time, (but "old" now) President of WSU, Lane Rawlins. Oh, and yes, there was one Husky there, Coach Jim Lambright. That was a super-special event. I tried to persuade them not to have the party. I'm glad they ignored me.

❧

Joan and Connie Gotzian, prominent Spokane friends and 100% Cougars, are unfailing in their support of every thing about WSU. These wonderful friends took good care of me in so many ways. They are among a rare breed of supporters who never complain nor criticize. If they have faith in you, they believe you will do the right thing. If they express a view about actions taken or decisions made, they do so in a way that you appreciate. They were thoughtful and generous. Often they invited me for the weekend to their beautiful, quiet home on Hayden Lake, particularly when I needed it most. And they didn't stop doing thoughtful and helpful things for me after I retired. That I especially appreciated. I'm glad they occasionally call me when they visit their children on Bainbridge Island.

Bob Hulbert, an alumnus and a very successful farmer from Skagit County, near Mt. Vernon, Washington, was extraordinarily helpful to WSU in the development and presentation of our budgets to the governor and the legislature. He was influential with the legislature because of his standing in the powerful statewide agricultural interests. However, his value to WSU extended beyond agriculture. He understands that the Federal Land Grant legislation specifically calls for a broad liberal arts background for agricultural and engineering programs. Consequently, he was an effective advocate for our total budget requests.

Bob came to the campus often on big weekends with Regents and Foundation meetings, and football games. On those occasions, he invariably brought beautiful flowers and berries from his farm for the Regents and me. Recently, he invited me to speak to the Alumni and Cougar Club annual meeting in Skagit County. Gail and I had fun being with the Hulberts and about one hundred other loyal boosters.

On one of the stops on my tour of the state after the demonstrations on campus, I met with the Colville Cattlemens' Association, and the Cowbelles, the womens counterpart organization. I had heard that many of our friends there were quite upset about what they had heard and read about the protestors' behavior on campus. I was expecting to be raked over the coals. We had a nice meal, and the time came for me to make a speech. I was pleasantly surprised to find that they listened attentively, asked a few questions in a very polite and cordial manner, and seemed to be satisfied with what I had to say.

After our discussion, several of the lady Cowbelles gave me an autographed book of recipes, naturally with beef as the main ingredient. I used that book often at the president's house, and it always brought back fond memories of my friends in Colville. This is but another experience that has lead me to believe that the WSU people are truly special. I think just the fact that I was there, giving them an opportunity to hear from and question me directly, gave them confidence in what we were attempting to accomplish at WSU.

Soon after the disturbance at the jail in Colfax described earlier, I met with citizens there in an attempt to help them gain a better general understanding of the activism phenomenon. They needed to know specifically what had happened to create the scene at the Colfax jail when Sheriff Humphrey attempted to jail the convicted students. Again, the citizens there seemed only to desire a meeting with me to hear what I had to say and to ask questions. And again, their treatment of me was civil, even cordial, for the most part. As was the case in Colville, there were no angry outbursts, only reasonable questions. I'm not saying that they agreed with me on all the actions we took, but most of them seemed to understand why we took the actions we did. That is remarkable, in view of the proximity of Colfax to Pullman, and the rumored threats of retaliations by vigilante groups in the Colfax area.

One day at noon I decided to have lunch with some students in the Coman dormitory. I went through the lunch line, and began to look for students who seemed to be receptive to my having lunch with them. Cathy Fort, a student seated at a table with several other students, saw me, and recognizing me, immediately, invited me to join their group. We had an interesting conversation, covering just about anything concerning life at WSU. That began a friendship with Cathy, which included an invitation to sing "The Lord's Prayer" at her wedding. I thanked her for thinking of me in such a great way, then tried to persuade her to engage another singer, since it had been many years since I had sung in a wedding. Cathy demonstrated a determined streak in her makeup that I had never observed before. She said she didn't care how out of singing shape I was, she wanted me to sing.

I respond well to strong women, especially if they are expressing confidence in me. So, I agreed to sing at Cathy's wedding. I practiced several times before the wedding hoping to regain some of my skills. Then during the ceremony, when my time to perform came, I rose to recognize the members of the wedding party, all of whom I knew, since they were all former WSU students. Much to my chagrin, I couldn't think of one student's name. Frustrated by failure to remember her name, l began to perform to the best of my ability. During my rendition, her name came to me, and I was so pleased that I stopped singing and called her name, Doreen, out loud, and then resumed singing to the end of "The Lord's Prayer." I've been prone to experience atrial fibrillation for thirty or more years, usually precipitated by excitement of some kind. I never mentioned this to Cathy, but I have not sung in a wedding since then, nor have I been invited to do so. That should tell me something.

◈

During my last year at WSU, I stopped by the football practice field to watch the student-athletes cavort. This was probably my last such visit, which explains what happened. As I approached the field, Reuben Mayes, Mark Ripien and Terry Porter, the famous RPM backfield, saw me and came running to greet me with a big hug. We chatted briefly, then they went back to their practice routine. I trudged off to do whatever I had to do, but with a jauntiness to my gait that wasn't there when I arrived at the practice field. Those young student-athletes had touched my heart with the warmth of their greeting.

◈

Clem and Jacquie Powell included me in many of their activities in the Seattle area, including hosting me in a game of golf at their beautiful course, Sahalee, where I embarrassed myself with the rustiness of my game. The Powells had me in their home for dinner, which I believe is one of the best things one can do for a friend. I vividly remember the first time I had ever been salmon fishing was with the Powells and other WSU friends. Of course, I became seasick. But I did not give in entirely to my misery. I had some friends alert me from a distance if a salmon got hooked on my line. One eager fish cooperated. I was alerted, and I jumped up, grabbed my gear and played the salmon half way around the boat and back before finally landing it. I then promptly returned to my prone position, but only after throwing up. Later, the Powells had a salmon bake at their home overlooking the Pacific Ocean. I learned that I much preferred eating salmon to fishing for them.

❧❦❧

The Gibb family from Bellingham, Washington are numerous: father, mother, brother, seven children, all attended WSU, and all enormously proud of that fact. Father Gibb, a doctor, brother Gibb, a swimming coach at WSU, Ruthie a marvelous mother, and the seven siblings, all talented and energetic. Dr. Bob was a fine Regent. He fought hard for his convictions, but if the majority of his fellow regents disagreed with him, he carried no resentment or hostile baggage around with him. Bob and Ruthie are generous to their school, making frequent donations, perhaps the most impressive of which are the two huge Cougars at the entrance of Beasley Coliseum.

❧❦❧

General Telephone Northwest Chief Executive Officer Al Barran invited me to become a member of their Board of Directors soon after I arrived at WSU. This appointment gave me an important contact with the business community in Washington, Idaho and Oregon. It was as a member of that board that I met other board members, prominent business men and women, which benefitted WSU. All of the GTE Board members were successful people, many in business throughout the Northwest. Harry Magnuson, from Wallace, Idaho became a good personal friend, not only of mine, but of WSU. He contributed generously to the scholarship created in my honor when I retired. Al Barran named the GTE Education Building, near Everett, Washington for me, which I appreciate immensely. Lee Coulter, general counselor is a great friend. GTE also made a generous contribution to the Terrell scholarship fund for students at WSU, in my opinion, one of the best programs one can support, especially in view of the steadily rising tuition and fees.

❧

Bob Smalley is a WSU legend. He was very helpful in providing information I needed for this book. He undoubtedly knows more about WSU history than anyone. He is a very talented speaker. His slide shows are both informative and funny. His sense of humor priceless. His slide presentations on special occasions like retirement functions make up for the often tediousness of the program. Bob has served WSU in many important roles, and his loyalty and continuing interest in his school are not exceeded by anyone, and matched by few.

❧

I have mentioned my assistant, Gen DeVleming earlier. She merits further recognition. First of all, she is very bright. Second, I trust her completely. She deserves that trust. She has the perfect trait of an associate, who would tell you what she thinks, but would support you all the way, whether or not the decision was consistent with her opinion. She is an authority on the strengths and weaknesses of presidents, since she "broke in" at least four and perhaps five of us. She has as much energy as anyone I have known, and she is fun to be with, at work or play.

❧

Sally Savage is a superb university lawyer. She understands that the university is her client. I know, technically, the Attorney General is also her client. Sally was never confused about these relationships. She just went about the business of serving WSU's legal needs. And not once did I question her judgment. Furthermore, she was great to work with, had a quick mind, and smiled and laughed freely. If not in title, Sally was an assistant to the president.

◈

Karen Brown Conley, a student in the 1970s, was one of my spiritual advisors, and a good one. She always had just the right thing to say that bolstered my spirits on the few times I needed that. She gave me a Bible, which I have used for many years. She was very fond of the Bentley, as were many students. Her father, Tex, is a loyal alumnus, and one of the first to become a member of the Presidents Associates of the WSU Foundation, those who donate at least one thousand dollars a year to the university. I don't see Karen and Jeff very often now, but when I do, it is always enjoyable.

◈

Jack Sutherland, former Alumni Association President, is especially remembered for his thoughtfulness in hosting me for lunch at the Tacoma Country Club. His only unthoughtful habit was his competitiveness and determination to beat me every time we played golf. And he always beat me. Jack's wife, Helen, was one of my defenders when I was being criticized for some decision I had made. Yes, the alumni, like the students and faculty members, took me seriously when I invited suggestions, even criticism. Helen was as nice a person as I have ever known.

◈

Bob Morgan, former Alumni Association President from Spokane, has taken good care of my meager investments for many years. University presidents in my days did not get those huge salaries and deferred benefits that are common today. Don't get me wrong, they earn every dollar of what they are getting, considering the heavy responsibilities they shoulder. But I was able to invest for the future, and Bob advised me wisely over the years. For that, I am very appreciative. I also remember his wife, Mary, and their children, especially the latter. One of their boys caught most of the salmon on the fishing trip referred to earlier, the one that kept me on my back most of the trip.

The Ministry of Leadership • 183

I remember Ed and Betty McWilliams from Spokane for many courtesies to me, and for Ed's value as a regent. Besides his intelligence, his sense of responsibility, and his sense of humor, he was an effective member of the team of regents at that time. He could be accounted on to inject humor into discussions that were beginning to be repetitious, or somewhat emotional. Ed keeps in touch often, which I appreciate.

Former student majors in Communications and Hotel and Restaurant Management have been a big part of my retirement years. Kathi Goertzen, Margo Myers, Bill Rixey, Enrique Cerna, Bill Yeend, Julia Sandstrom and other Cougars dominate TV and radio. I see and hear them almost daily, and that is joyful.

During my tenure at WSU, Pat Foley, the leader of the Hyatt Hotels, Warren Anderson, manager of The Olympic Hotel in Seattle and the Davenport in Spokane, Harry Mullikin, Westin Hotel's leader in Seattle, along with numerous others along the West coast, were WSU alumni that I saw frequently. Since I no longer have frequent need of hotel accommodations, nor do Gail and I eat out often, I am not in as close touch with our Hotel and Restaurant leaders as I once was. I do know that in Seattle, Tom Norwalk has risen rapidly in the ranks of hotel management leaders, and that Annie Holbrook is now working at the Seattle Sheraton Hotel. Also, among the more recent graduates, Paul Ishii manages the Mayflower Hotel with skill and poise. We had an excellent dinner there recently, and he could not have been more hospitable.

Former Cougar athletes are also quite visible in Seattle. The Seahawks have Chad Eaton, Robbie Tobeck, and Rian Lindell. Unfortunately, the Seahawks are not winning, but they will soon. Playing for the Mariners is John Olerud, in my opinion, their best player. James Donaldson, a fine basketball player recruited by George Raveling, is a neighbor in Magnolia. It is good to see him often on my daily walks. Joe McIntosh, an excellent pitcher for the Cougars in the 1970s, is John Olerud's attorney. Joe played for the San Diego Padres. He recently gave me a baseball, autographed by John Olerud, to give to a boy who is gravely ill. If that isn't great Cougar spirit, what is? Thank you, Joe and John!

⟡

Darwin and Sherry Cook bring special memories to mind. We became good friends following the tragic death of one of their daughters in an automobile accident. Losing students caused me intense grief. We had a memorial service, and of course Sherry and Darwin were there on campus. That was the beginning of a very good friendship. They, along with the Beasleys and Brunstads, had an annual salmon barbeque in Port Ludlow for many years for all the Cougars who lived on the Peninsula, and for the Regents who met in a western Washington community during the summer. Sherry is an expert quilter. She did me the honor of making a quilt of Cougar colors with a Cougar logo in the middle which I cherish. They now live in Skamania, Washington. They are better than I am about keeping in touch, but no better about thinking of me than I am of them.

⟡

Jack and Catherine Friel are legends in Pullman. Jack was a great basketball coach and the court in Beasley Coliseum was named for him. I have vivid memories of their attending functions where I was also in attendance. Catherine always made a bee-line for me, to either congratulate me or correct me for something I had done that displeased her. Jack would stand by shaking his head. He didn't quite understand that I enjoyed every encounter with Catherine. She was and I'm sure still is what I would call charmingly aggressive. I was told by Bob Smalley that Catherine recently had her one hundredth birthday. I'm confident that she is as sharp as ever. I hope she buys a copy of this book.

⟡

Mary Lou LaPiere was very effective as head of WSU West. In our many conversations about WSU in general and about the Foundation, I found her to be insightful, knowledgeable and loyal. I recommended her as a consultant for Panarama City, the retirement community in Lacey, Washington. (I serve on their Corporate Board). She assisted us in the establishment of a foundation, and in the recruitment of a Director of Development. She did an exceptional job, and was liked by all who worked with her. Furthermore, the person she recommended as Director is doing an excellent job. Thank you, Mary Lou. Also, it was good to see you and Jack Dillon at my eightieth birthday party.

❦

Edie Williams, granddaughter of President Teddy Roosevelt, was a fine Regent. She knitted me a Cougar pillow cover which I cherish. As a Regent, she also said what she thought about issues, but always in a nice, cultured way. And she was a team player, which is very important, since Regents derive their legal influence and authority as a group. She never pouted if she didn't get her way. She moved on to the next issue, which is also very important for Regents. She was always thoughtful to me, and the other Regents.

❦

Kate Webster was as capable as a regent as she was a hostess and cook. I could not say anything more complimentary than that. She frequently had the regents and me to dinner at her home on Bainbridge Island. And we were always greeted warmly by her Airdale companion. He looked big enough to eat you, but fortunately, he was as hospitable as Kate. Kate's strength as a Regent was her ability to listen to all sides of complicated issues, and change her mind, if the information we gave her was persuasive enough.

One of my goals in writing this book is to acknowledge in sufficiently emphatic ways the good fortune I had at WSU in having excellent, supportive regents. Without that support from all of them, my tenure would have been much shorter, either because I would have been replaced or I would have quit. Despite the many mistakes I made, a university benefits from effective working and personal relationships. As mentioned earlier, a president is useless if the regents don't have confidence in him/her.

Paul Castleberry, a professor of Political Science wrote me a letter I shall never forget. I was one of the finalists for the chancellorship at the University of California in San Diego. He expressed a hope that I would remain at WSU, that many challenges remained to be met there. Those thoughtful words influenced my decision to withdraw from further consideration at San Diego. I have never regretted that decision. Incidentally, I will also always remember Paul's oratory in faculty meetings. They were most memorable. And it was good to observe that Paul enjoyed them too.

Bill Bigger, now a resident in a retirement community in the Seattle area, lived in California for a significant part of his life. He never failed to participate in the frequent alumni events in southern California. He also frequently arranged golf games while I was there, and invited me to dinner at his home. Bill was a witness to one of my red-letter days when I chipped in from just off the green three times during an eighteen hole match. That is the only time I've ever done that, and don't expect to do it again.

Paula Symbol Spence, an alumna from Seattle, and her father, Paul Symbol, also a Cougar, have been good friends since Paula was a student. Our friendship has carried over from her college days. I see them both on occasion, and we have dinner whenever Gail's and my schedules, and theirs permit it. Paula is lending support in the book project, and is giving me marketing ideas. Paula is the kind of friend who worries about you if she thinks you are not paying enough attention to safety issues. For example, she arrived for dinner at our home one evening lugging two 5-gallon jugs of water for us to have on hand in case of an earthquake. Thank you, Paula, for caring.

Bill and Jean Lane, California residents, and owners and publishers of Sunset Magazine, have a son, Bob, who attended WSU, and like many Californians, loved our school. When parents have a son or daughter who likes life as a Cougar, more often than not the parents also like WSU. And such is the case with the Lanes. They visited the campus often when Bob was a student. They occasionally were guests at the president's house. They were very nice, and interesting, and became good personal friends. Often when we had functions in the Bay Area of California, they hosted our group in fine style at their elegant headquarters facility. I consider them honorary alumni. In fact, they had a retirement function for me which was held in conjunction with a Foundation meeting in 1985. Our relationships with these great friends illustrates the value to parents in having their son or daughter happy and successful. From a university relations standpoint, nothing is more important.

⚜

Alumni, Jan (ladies first, Ron) and Ron Pickering have also supported me totally. There must have been times when they disagreed with some of the decisions I made, but if they did, I did not know about it. It made no difference in our relationship. They had me to dinner often, which was a treat, since Jan is a great culinary artist. I was always impressed that Ron was a good helper. Ron transported me to Pullman for football games occasionally when I moved to Seattle in 1987. No friends have been more thoughtful to me than the Pickerings, nor more faithful in their devotion to WSU.

⚜

Chas and Bea Nagel were and still are special friends. They are as dedicated to WSU as anybody. I have attempted to persuade them to move to the Seattle area without success, indeed without their willingness to even discuss the idea. So I have resorted to the telephone to keep in touch. Friendship is important to our continuing to keep in touch. Bea's encyclopedic knowledge of activities going on in Pullman is another powerful factor. Her narrative skill still another. When Gail hears me laughing while talking on the phone, she knows it's Bea on the other end of the line. Walter Clore and Chas have been leaders in the development of the wine industry in Washington State. Chas has been a guiding light for many in the wine industry in the Northwest.

⁓ঌ৵⁓

Keith Jackson, the best sportscaster ever, was mentioned earlier in connection with the interview on television at the Stanford football game during my first year at WSU. Keith was enormously helpful in getting the WSU Foundation started, and in contributing time, effort and money in the earlier years. He is still devoting time, thought and money to our continuing success. Keith is also an accomplished speaker and raconteur.

⁓ঌ৵⁓

Another Keith is Keith Lincoln, our Alumni Director. I mentioned Keith earlier in connection with his good work with the alumni regarding the decision to replace Butch with a student-cougar mascot. He has been an effective Alumni Director in every respect. He is a team player, as are all great football players. In his football playing days, he was one of the real heroes I had. I watched him on television regularly. He certainly was one the most versatile players, running, receiving, and kicking. And he is a Cougar through and through.

⁓ঌ৵⁓

Marge and Stan Coe who have led the Alumni Association, rented a duplex to me in Magnolia when I moved to Seattle. Stan has taken good care of our dogs, and on occasion, all too infrequently, Marge has provided us an excellent dinner. Stan, normally an easy-going person, demonstrated a firmness on at least one occasion when the Alumni Association was having a party at Ste. Michelle Winery. Stan and I wanted to tell the members how bleak the legislative appropriations outlook was, and to enlist their help in lobbying Olympia for better treatment. We had some difficulty getting their attention. The wine may have had much to do with that. At that time, Stan was the President of the Association, and felt responsible for their inattention. He let them know of his displeasure in no uncertain terms, not only with the tone of his voice, but also with his red face and body language. That did it. I never saw them more attentive the rest of that or any other evening.

The Ministry of Leadership • 189

Al Heglund, an alumnus in Seattle and a very successful business man, started the first WSU West campus in his office many years before there was an official office. Many of us used it, including myself. Al had long advocated an expansion of WSU activities and programs in Seattle, and typical for Al, he offered a separate section of his office for that purpose. He had many good ideas for support programs, and he rightfully believed that our presence in Seattle was inadequate. He was right. I believe that concern by some over how the University of Washington would react to such a development was the primary reason why we did not start this sooner.

Nancy Brown, an alumna from Wenatchee, was at WSU during the student unrest period. We had frequent conversations about the issues that generated the protests. She had the intelligence and the interest in the social issues of that time, which led her to attend some of the demonstrations. After some of them, she engaged me in conversations. I always enjoyed those talks. Our friendship led her to bring apples and pears often when she came to Pullman for football games. Her father and mother were among the first WSU alums I met when I came to Pullman in 1967. I am pleased that we have continued to be friends. She is among the numerous alums who sent me an email encouraging me to write this book.

Ed Bennett, professor of History, besides being a good scholar, also served WSU very well as our faculty representative to the Pac-10 Conference. Ed had the respect of his colleagues on the WSU faculty as well as the faculties of other member universities. The best thing that can be said to support that statement is that we did not break any major rules of the Conference or the National Collegiate Athletic Association while Ed was "standing guard." There were a few minor problems, like inadvertently playing a non-eligible athlete for a game, but nothing that embarrassed me or the university, or that resulted in heavy penalties. We are indebted to Ed for this important service.

❧

Charlie Drake, a professor of Bacteriology was a hunter, a pilot, and a gourmet. He and Audrey invited me to dinner occasionally. Anyone who knew Charlie knows that these dinners were not only delicious but were accompanied by many stories of his hunting and flying expeditions, often with Herb Eastlick. I can't believe that Herb got in Charlie's airplane, so maybe I'm wrong about that. Anyway, I remember distinctly that they hunted together. The last time I remember seeing Charlie and Audrey was at a Gilbert and Sullivan event in Seattle. He was a fan of G&S, a fact that establishes Charlie as having broad interests. As I remember, he sold his excellent homemade bread to Pullman restaurants. That's probably why I don't remember his ever giving me any, except when he served it in his home.

❧

Rich Meyer was President of the Graduate Student Association during the demonstrations. He was a stable influence on the campus. I detected leadership traits in his make-up. It was obvious that Rich was going to be successful in whatever he decided to focus on as a career. His field was food and nutrition. His talents did not go undetected. Early in his career, he became Vice President of Research at Nalleys, a position he held for quite a few years. He now has his own company, and continues to be successful. We keep in touch regularly.

I remember vividly when he and his wife came to my office to tell me that they were going to Ithaca, New York, where he had been accepted at Cornell University's doctoral program in nutrition. They then told me that his wife had not been successful in being admitted to Cornell. She was an excellent student. I then called Al Baldwin, a friend and a distinguished professor in the department where she had applied. I told Professor Baldwin that he was making a mistake not to admit Rich's wife. He reconsidered and admitted her. She is now a recognized scholar. Rich and his wife Rosie occasionally have dinner with Gail and me.

☙❧

The Clark family in Pullman, including the prominent State Senator, Ace, his sons, Asa and Gerard, and their families were among the most supportive friends I had. I thank them for that.

☙❧

I must mention the Goldsworthy family, including sons, Harry, an Air Force General, and Bob, an excellent State Representative. Both are loyal Cougars, and Bob, the respected legislator, was always helpful with WSU's budget requests. His sense of humor made my budget presentations enjoyable. Anyone who can do that has talent.

☙❧

Elmer Huntley, WSU's State Senator, was as helpful as anyone could be. He frequently visited me in Pullman, offering to be of help in legislation affecting WSU. What a great friend and gentleman he was.

☙❧

Pat Patterson, could not have been more supportive, with the legislature, and as Keith Lincoln's predecessor, served the Alumni Association with loyalty and tenacity.

☙❧

Gene Prince was also helpful with legislature. Thank you, Gene.

☙❧

Marshall Neill: State Senator, Federal Judge in Spokane, legal advisor to the WSU Board of Regents and loyal alumnus. The Neill family members have been intimately involved in WSU and Pullman history since the early days. I feel very fortunate to have had several years' experience working with this distinguished leader.

☙❧

The Caraher family, including Joe, two term President of the Alumni Association, Marcella, his wife, and son, Pat, the Editor of the Washington State University Magazine, have given strong, informed support to our university in many ways. Joe is the superb publisher of the Klamath Falls, Oregon newspaper. Pat learned about journalism from an early age.

Paul Allen was a student when I was at WSU. We were not acquainted, a slip up for me, but we are happy to claim him as one of ours. Paul has generously modernized much of WSU's computer capability, for which we are most appreciative.

Dallas Barnes is remembered for his excellent work during the unrest era for his deep sense of responsibility and for his skill working with students and faculty of various cultures. An African-American, Dallas enjoyed the respect of all of us from different backgrounds.

Wendell Gray was also an effective colleague during the campus unrest period. Unfortunately, he died at a very early age. I went to Alabama to visit with his mother. It was a very sad experience for me, but he was worthy of being included in this book.

To those of you whose name has not been included in this book, I express profound gratitude for supporting and believing in me, each in your own special way. Every one of you helped make my years at WSU and since then, the experience of a lifetime.

Chapter Fourteen
LIFE AFTER THE PRESIDENCY: THE PACIFIC INSTITUTE

Earlier in this book, I referred to my affiliation with The Pacific Institute, an educational corporation with offices in several foreign nations, including the U.K., Australia, South Africa and Japan, in addition to the headquarters in Seattle. Over thirty years ago, Lou and Diane Tice established the company. As mentioned earlier, the company offers programs and consulting services to organizations and individuals, that are designed to enable them to perform as close to their capability as possible.

The content of the programs relies on the research findings of leading scholars in cognitive psychology, including: Albert Bandura, of Stanford University; Martin Seligman, of the University of Pennsylvania; Gary Latham, at the University of Toronto; and the work of many others, including the students and other devotees of Bandura, Seligman and Latham. All of them occupy distinguished Chairs at their universities and each has been heavily involved in leadership positions in psychology. Both Seligman and Bandura have served as President of the American Psychological Association, and Latham as President of the Canadian Psychological Association. All have authored many books and articles in professional journals. Bandura's most comprehensive recent book is *Self-Efficacy: The Exercise of Control.* This book contains reviews of much of his research, as well as research of others in support of social-cognitive theory on the facilitating effect of one's own thought control on human performance. In Bandura's theory and book, thought control refers to one's own thought control. Self- Efficacy is defined as the *belief* that one can establish and attain goals of one's own choice.

The Pacific Institute applies the findings of Bandura, Seligman, Latham and others to our work with clients, helping them to reach optimal performance. We are not a motivation company. One could say that we provide instruction to our clients that enables *them* to motivate themselves by the use of cognitive skills (thinking skills) that help them to develop, in Banduran terms, self-efficacy. Remarkable increases in performance follow increases in self-efficacy and collective or organization efficacy. The cognitive skills we teach to improve efficacy include goal-setting, self-talk, affirmations, scotomas, possibility thinking — somewhat similar to the cognitive skills involved in learning the contrarian thinking style, as defined by President Steven Sample, of the University of Southern California, discussed earlier. Professor Bandura has developed the general framework of Efficacy Theory. Seligman's focus is on self-talk, or as he calls it, *explanatory style* (the way one explains a successful or a failure experience to one's self). Latham's emphasis is on goal-setting, particularly in organizational performance evaluation.

Our client base is extensive. We have worked with many Fortune 500 companies, including financial, high tech, retail, manufacturing companies as well as local, state and federal agencies, hospitals, the military, schools and universities, and law enforcement agencies. For many years, WSU used trained facilitators to administer the centerpiece program, *Investment in Excellence®*, to staff personnel. Dr. Bob Wilson has used it with faculty and students in the College of Veterinary Medicine. We are now using the program in the K-12 educational system, in addition to the other types of client organizations listed above. The basic program has been adapted to many of our clients to make it more specific to their needs.

The Pacific Institute helps some clients develop measurement instruments to determine the outcomes of our work with them, although we encourage them to engage a third party to conduct the outcome studies. We also have many convincing testimonials from our clients, about the value of our work on productivity, teamwork, employer-employee relationships, and even about improved family relationships. In order to be in any business for thirty years, customers must be satisfied. And most of ours are satisfied.

My role in the company is to connect them with the academic world with scholars like Bandura, Seligman, and Latham, who have all presented their work to The Pacific Institute. It is my responsibility to keep them informed about other current research findings related to our work and to assist them in designing measuring instruments. I also edit a periodical, *The LETTER*, which contains reports from our clients, and reviews of recent publications. The work is very interesting and important. Lou and Diane Tice are very bright and creative, and have become close personal friends. I've never observed a better teacher-presenter than Lou, and I have seen many in my long lifetime. Diane's marvelous spirit permeates the company. Jack Fitterer, the nephew of Father Jack Fitterer the former president of Seattle University, is President, and, among numerous other duties, is the financial leader of the company. The staff people who are attracted to the work of the company are committed to the social service thrust of the organization. We help our clients in numerous ways that are very gratifying. It has similarities to my description of the ministry work of the university presidency. We see the effects of our work in improved performance of our customers and the happiness they experience in improved human relationships.

Because Bandura's social cognitive theory is of great importance to the mission of The Pacific Institute, I am including my review of his book *Self-Efficacy: The Exercise of Control* in Appendix B.

The power of a psychological theory is determined by the degree which it predicts behavior. Bandura's book, *Self-Efficacy*, demonstrates the range of behavior predicted by this theory.

Post Script

The transition experience from the presidency to a different life after the presidency can be difficult at first. I knew that I wanted to do something that I believed to be important, but I made the mistake of not planning ahead for what that would be. Strangely, I didn't realize that there are two stages to retirement: Stage One is to stop what you are doing, and Stage Two is to decide what you want to do thereafter. I made the first stage easily, despite the difficulties of not seeing many friends as often as before.

I remember talking to Charles Odegaard about retirement. One thing he said stuck with me: "Whatever you do now is up to you. Don't expect it to be any other way." He was right, as he was about so many things during his fifteen year term as president of the University of Washington. My work with The Pacific Institute provided a superb transition from the presidency. I hope that all of you who have not yet retired will be as fortunate as I have been with my life at WSU and after retirement, at The Pacific Institute.

STUDY COUNCIL REPORT SUMMARIES

I agreed with the General Education Council's recommendation that a separate college of General Education, with a budget of its own, would increase the probability that the concept of general education, representing all disciplines, would be strengthened. I regret that this recommendation was not implemented. Also important is the insistence of the General Education group that academic advisors be chosen "with great care." The recommendations for the establishment of Research Institutes, or appropriate name changes in existing institutes, is an important goal for a university seeking to enhance its research capability. The evolution of the name of the Institute, or Social and Economic Science Research Center is an excellent example, since it provides an entity that serves the research needs for all the social sciences.

Among the recommendations of the Council on Engineering is the following quote: "We also conclude that the strengthening of the graduate program is the most critical problem facing the College of Engineering." Also stressed was the high priority of preparing students for jobs in engineering, immediately upon graduation. I remember many practicing engineers frequently telling me that our students were well-prepared for jobs, in fact better prepared than those from another university in the state of Washington. Historically, the mission of Engineering at the University of Washington has been directed more toward the preparation of students for graduate degrees and careers in research. (I interpreted the recommendation of the study council to contain a greater emphasis on graduate education and research in the years ahead for WSU.)

Again, quoting from the Council on Biological Sciences report, "Strong support of a graduate program attracts and retains a research-oriented faculty consisting of substantial scholars. Such a faculty attracts the most talented students and obtains the most money from external sources to support research and training. We trust that it will be obvious that we recommend the development of this course of action at a rate that does not jeopardize the support of the undergraduate curricula."

The statement from the report of the Council on Agriculture, which got my attention, follows. "The shortage of trained personnel in scientific agriculture and related industries requires not only a new look at the university undergraduate curriculum, but also increased attention to graduate training. Industry and government are taking an increased amount of people with graduate degrees in agricultural sciences. The demand of extension, research and teaching for persons with advanced degrees has vastly increased in twenty years. Our international programs have added to this demand. Therefore the unique contribution of land-grant universities in the field of graduate training should be recognized and strengthened at once."

The first recommendation mentioned by the Economics and Business Administration Council was, and I quote, "The graduate programs in the College of Economics and Business should receive increased emphasis. . .We believe that the departments in the College of Economics and Business should be supported when they find it possible and desirable to strengthen their graduate programs by hiring senior faculty members." Another recommendation was for the establishment of a doctoral program in Business Administration, established a few years later. As mentioned above, the Economics and Business and the Social Science Councils collaborated in the development of a Social and Economic Science Research Center.

The Study Council on Home Economics appears to give equal weight to undergraduate and graduate education. The statement that best represents the thrust of the Council's report is as follows: "The key to the future growth and development of the departments in this college rests with the nature of the research and graduate program. This will largely determine the quality of all future endeavors. It is recognized that this has been relatively weak, and therefore most resources should be focused on strengthening these programs."

The Humanities Study Council focused on the lack of support for disciplines in the humanities, as compared to other disciplines, not only at WSU, but also in terms of federal and foundation support. Such claims are true and understandable. The report makes a series of recommendations, most of which involve increased support for faculty salaries, library and physical accommodations. As I read the Humanities report, I cringe at the thought that I may not have addressed the Humanities disciplines as vigorously as I did other needs of the university. For that, I am profoundly sorry.

The Physical Sciences Council report begins with a statement of general priorities as follows: The education of students with a "serious interest in science," those with a "peripheral interest in science," "research beneficial to the state," and "other professional activities." Specific recommendations include the further development of chemical physics, biochemistry, and geophysics. These programs exist to benefit undergraduate and graduate students. The report seems to give equal attention to both undergraduate and graduate students. A key quote for emphasis on research is, "The central theme of Ph.D. programs in the natural sciences is scholarly research. The value of teaching is emphasized by the equal weight they give to publications and teaching skills."

It appeared to me that the Off-Campus Cooperative Extension Council's main concern was the lack of coordination in the total extension programs at WSU. It was clear that this was a serious problem in 1967. The Council recommended the creation of a central administration office led by a vice-president reporting directly to the president, so that WSU's responsibility as a land-grant university could be effectively discharged. Most of their report, in one form or another, seemed to be related to the lack of a highly placed visible office with responsibility for bringing together the departments of the entire university to address the issues and problems of the state.

The Off Campus Research Council presented an interesting list of accomplishments covering much of the application of research findings that have made the United States a leader in supplying food for the entire world. This type of research is often labeled "mission-oriented" research. The first recommendation of the Council is that we designate mission-oriented research as a "prime objective" for the future. Some specific suggestions which flow from this prime objective include the following: Encourage fundamental research in solving problems; develop computer capability for storing and retrieving important data; a system for keeping faculty up to date on new discoveries; develop regional agricultural centers; and the creation of an agricultural fund to support faculty research in promising fields.

The report of the Study Council for Mathematics is missing about ten pages. Obviously, this means that my comments will be limited to the report from pages 11 through 54. The report contained important information about multiple sections of some courses in introductory mathematics. One issue addressed is the challenge of the differences in preparation of the graduate student instructors. It is suggested that greater attention be focused on more uniformity of instruction and in assessment of student performance. The uneven quality of teaching by graduate instructors is a perennial problem, and is rightfully mentioned by the Council.

The Study Council for Mathematics dwells at some length on graduate instruction. I quote from this report: "Vigorous scholarship of a rather narrow type is an essential prerequisite of a successful graduate program. Both the Department of Mathematics and the program in Information Science have the philosophy of attempting to cultivate special strength against a background of sound overall coverage." Other issues discussed are the department's commitment to providing mathematics and statistics to other departments and graduate students. Finally, the report recommends a Department of Statistics.

The Study Council on Professional Education consisted of reports of subcommittees from Veterinary Medicine and Pharmacy. Much of the report of the College of Veterinary Medicine consisted of recommendations for extensive infusions of support in faculty positions, equipment and facilities, in order to regain accreditation lost a few years earlier. It is a great source of satisfaction that we were able to remove the deficiencies, and become one the best colleges of Veterinary Medicine in the nation. The recommendations of the Study Council were sound, and provided us with a blueprint of what was needed. The importance of the leadership of Leo Bustad, the dean of the college, cannot be overstated.

The College of Pharmacy joined the College of Veterinary Medicine in recommending salary improvements for both colleges in order to compete with other universities for the best available faculty members. The Council also recommended that additional space in the east wing of College Hall be assigned to the college.

A few years after the Study Councils reported, and we began to implement some of the recommendations, a dark cloud descended on the College of Pharmacy in the form of a recommendation from the Council on Higher Education. This coordinating agency for higher education came forth with what was the most foolish recommendation in their checkered history – the elimination of WSU's College of Pharmacy! They had little or no grasp of the trouble that would cause them if they persisted in this ridiculous plan. In the first place, the College of Pharmacy had no difficulty gathering data to demonstrate that the State of Washington needed two colleges of Pharmacy. Secondly, the Council on Higher Education, at that time a political creature, did not have the faintest grasp of the politics of their recommendation.

The whole affair was worrisome, even though I had no doubt that we could help them change their position without resorting to political means. The small communities of Washington would have none of this idea. They rightfully pointed out to the Council on Higher Education that for many years they relied on pharmacists from the WSU College of Pharmacy, and that such a move would be detrimental to the well-being of their communities. Dean Larry Simonsmeier was extraordinarily effective in developing the strategy for disputing the claims of the Council on Higher Education that the State did not need two Colleges of Pharmacy.

The Social Sciences Study Council recommendations, like those of other Councils, gave equal attention to undergraduate and graduate program needs. The first recommendation was the immediate establishment of a program in Asian languages, recommended also by the Ad Hoc Committee Report on International Programs. Among other recommendations were that consideration be given to instituting more five-hour courses and fewer three-hour courses, so that the student be given the experience of delving more deeply into disciplines than three-hour courses permit. The Council also recommended that graduate fellowships be allocated in order to compete more successfully for the top graduate students. Another significant recommendation of the Social Science Council was for the establishment of an Institute of Applied Social Research, which, as mentioned earlier, evolved into the current Social and Economic Science Research Center.

The Study Council on Teacher Education, through its subcommittees, recommended the following: improve interdepartmental communication. To make this possible, one staff member in all departments involved in teacher education should be responsible for communication with the College of Education. Also recommended was an all-university Council on Teacher Preparation. The Study Council was in total agreement on this suggestion, even though it was divided about the exact duties of this body. Also recommended was the equal value of teaching and research in faculty evaluations. Foresight was involved in the recommendation of live, closed-circuit television classes with connections to any school in the United States. Finally, a minority report expresses regret that there is a split between what is referred to as academic faculty and teacher education faculty, regarding the importance of teacher education.

The Student Life Study Council stressed the preliminary nature of their report, and that the suggestions and recommendations made are not those of the Council as a whole, but of the six sub-councils: Student Profile, The Learning Process, Student Government and Student Role in Decision-Making, Social and Recreational Facilities, Housing, and Student Health and Safety.

The sub-committee on Student Profile points out that the university did not have enough information about its students, and that the UCLA research on national profiles, though helpful in some respects, is limited in its help for WSU's needs. The Student Government and Role in Decision-Making reported, after extensive interviews, that there was a serious communication gap between all components of the university. Further, this group reported that the most serious problem with student government was the students' lack of confidence in their own system of government, especially their feeling that the system does not represent the students' needs effectively. Again, the feeling of the students was that there was a lack of effective communication between students and their representatives. This was valuable information when attempting to better understand the root causes of the activism period at WSU, which started less than a year after the Study Council reports.

The LETTER: Book Review

Self-Efficacy: The Exercise of Control by Albert Bandura

This book is considered by some as the author's *magnum opus,* his greatest work. It clearly is his synthesis of more than 20 years of research related to his well known social-cognitive theory, in which the concepts of self-efficacy, forethought, human agency and self-regulation play central roles. Because of the great importance of Bandura's theory and research to the structure and content of The Pacific Institute's curriculum, this review will be extensive so TPI personnel will have an overview of the theory, and its many applications, related to the client groups we serve around the world.

A glance at the Table of Contents reveals what this reviewer believes to be the most valuable contribution of *Self-Efficacy:* the power of Bandura's theory as revealed by his research and that of many others working within his social-cognitive framework. The power of a psychological theory is simply the degree to which the theory predicts behavior. Aside from the first three or four chapters (which consist, for the most part, of an explanation of his efficacy theory, its sources and processes), the book covers the specific behaviors and benefits which are largely determined by perceived self-efficacy: school performance, behavior throughout the life cycle (early childhood, adolescence, mid-life and the elderly), health benefits, and clinical, athletic and organizational applications. The last chapter is devoted to collective efficacy, Bandura's most detailed and systematic treatment of this exceedingly important extension of individual efficacy.

It is important to distinguish between self-efficacy and two other concepts frequently used by behavior scientists: self-concept and self-esteem. Bandura defines self-efficacy as "belief in one's capabilities to organize and execute the courses of action required to produce given attainments," or in TPI's language, the belief that one can set and reach one's goals. Bandura's definition of self-concept is "a composite view of oneself." Bandura further differentiates self-efficacy from self-esteem with this statement: "Perceived self-efficacy is concerned with judgments of personal capability, whereas self-esteem is concerned with judgments of self-worth." Bandura further states that, "There is no fixed relationship between beliefs about one's capabilities and whether one likes or dislikes oneself." This reviewer thinks of self-esteem as a by product of perceived self-efficacy.

As mentioned above, the terms *human agency, self-regulation* and *forethought* are also important in Bandura's theory. Human agency refers to those unique personal skills, such as thought, that are essential for human beings to contribute substantially to their future. Forethought is also essentially a skill unique to the human species and refers to the ability to anticipate the future and to use cognitive skills, such as affirmations and self-talk, that will assist in controlling the future. Finally, self-regulation, or the ability to control one's behavior, is a by-product of perceived self-efficacy.

From the above, it is clear that efficacy theory is a formulation that predicts the control that human beings yearn for in all aspects of their lives, the control that enables them to set and reach goals and to perform at a level commensurate with their potential. We at The Pacific Institute teach the skills that are necessary to the attainment of high self-efficacy. It follows that Bandura's theory and research, which have received widespread attention throughout the world, are such an important scientific foundation for the programs of The Pacific Institute. For this reason, it is recommended that everyone associated with The Pacific Institute have a copy of *Self-Efficacy* in his or her personal library, to be used primarily as a reference book. This will be easy since there are three extensive alphabetical indices: author, name and subject. (For example, to find discussions in the book on self-esteem, guided mastery or modeling, simply refer to the subject index. To find research performed by Seligman, refer to the name index.)

Health Benefits of Perceived Self-Efficacy

Much research has been done with animal and human subjects showing the adverse effects of stress on physiological processes. For obvious reasons some of this research cannot be done on human subjects. (Some even oppose the use of animals.) Bandura devised a remedy for this problem by using subjects with pre-existing phobic conditions and giving mastery experience designed to provide a sense of coping efficacy which eliminated the stress. All subjects were eventually given the mastery experience. As Bandura states, "The findings of these experiments reveal that perceived coping efficacy operates as a critical cognitive mediator of biological stress reactions." The biological stress reactions used were variations of heart-rate and blood pressure. It is important to note that it is not the stress itself but the perceived inability to manage the stress that creates the adverse reactions in the cardiovascular system.

From this and similar studies, Bandura concludes that, "Effective self regulation is not achieved through an act of will. It requires the development of self-regulatory skills. Once empowered with skills and belief in their capabilities [the cognitive skills that we at TPI teach], people are better able to choose behaviors that facilitate the acquisition of self-regulation skills and to eliminate those that impair it. A growing body of evidence reveals that the impact of therapeutic interventions on health behavior is partly mediated by their effects on efficacy beliefs. This has been shown in studies conducted in such diverse areas of health as enhancement of pulmonary function in patients suffering from chronic obstructive pulmonary disease; recovery of cardiovascular function in post-coronary patients; reduction of pain and dysfunction in rheumatoid arthritis; amelioration of tension headaches; control of labor and childbirth pain; management of chronic lower back, neck and leg pain and impairment; stress reduction; weight reduction; exercise of control over bulimic behavior; reduction of cholesterol through dietary means; adherence to a regular program of physical exercise; maintenance of diabetic self-care; successful coping with painful invasive medical procedures; effective management of sexual coercion and contraceptives used to avoid unwanted pregnancies; post-abortion adjustment; control of sexual practices that pose high risk for transmission of AIDS; and control of addictive habits that impair health such as alcohol abuse, smoking and use of opiate drugs." The fact that efficacy predicts such a broad range of health-related behaviors underscores the enormous power of self-efficacy theory.

Development of Self-Efficacy

Bandura presents an interesting description and analysis of the development of self-efficacy throughout the life cycle, from early childhood through advanced age, emphasizing the adaptive character of human agency at each development level. Infants learn that they have the power to control their immediate environment through their own actions, or as Bandura would put it, through their *agency*. The development of language rapidly accelerates this learning of self-efficacy. Bandura further emphasizes the importance of parents providing the infant and preschool child with experiences that contribute to perceived self-efficacy, such as providing mastery and modeling experiences, encouragement through reading and time spent through activities that require thinking skills. The skills learned through such activities carry over into adolescence and adulthood.

Bandura stresses the life-long learning of one's perceived efficacy, with each level of development contributing uniquely to this process. For example, in adolescence, the influence of the peer group and the school are powerful forces in the attainment of efficacy, which in turn greatly affects the choice of friends, school performance, decisions of lifestyle and subsequently the choice of careers. Significantly, research shows that programs involving instruction in self-regulation decreases the probability that individuals will engage in risky drug and sexual behavior, whereas just teaching the facts of the possible consequences of risky behavior has little impact.

Predictably, the role of effective self-regulation in extending effective cognitive functioning during the later years of life is considerable. In a study by Bandura and others, four factors were found to determine whether or not the elderly continue to experience effective cognitive functioning: A sense of efficacy to influence events in one's life; educational level; physically active life style; and pulmonary capacity. Also, much recent research shows that memory can actually be improved in the later years. Interestingly, if the elderly believe they can improve their memory, they will do so.

Cognitive Functioning

In this chapter, Bandura discusses the interrelationships between perceived self-efficacy and numerous other variables on performance in a variety of tasks. One important study shows the interaction of perceived mathematics efficacy and ability on mathematics performance. The figure to the right shows that for students of low, medium and high ability, those with high efficacy in mathematics perform at a significantly higher level than those with low efficacy. Interesting, the chart

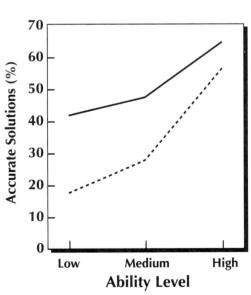

also shows that the importance of self-efficacy on performance decreases as ability level increases.

In another somewhat more complicated study by Bandura and others, represented by the figure below, we see the influence of perceived self-efficacy and parents' and children's academic aspi-

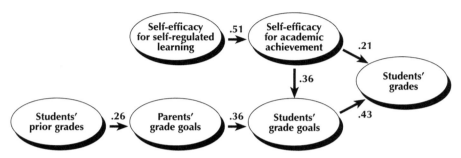

rations on children's academic achievement. The numbers above the lines connecting the variables shown indicate correlation between the variables. For example, the correlation between self-regulated learning and self-efficacy for academic achievement is .51; between self-efficacy for academic achievement and student's grade goals is .36 and so on. It is important to note that efficacy beliefs have both direct and indirect (through raising personal goals) effects on achievement. The analysis of Cognitive Functioning in various settings would not be complete without at least a reference to the importance of perceived self-efficacy in the performance of more complicated tasks. Studies have shown that learning in graduate colleges is more effective when the beliefs of personal efficacy are higher. In fact, Bandura asserts that self-efficacy "has a substantially greater impact on academic performance than the personal, social, and occupational outcomes," and that "perceived academic efficacy plays an influential role in career choice and development. It predicts academic grades, the range of career options considered, and persistence and success in chosen fields." Other studies show that perceived efficacy is exceedingly important in creative work.

Clinical Applications

Bandura discusses clinical applications of his human agency theory to psychological problems, including phobias, anxiety, depression, eating disorders and drug and alcohol dependency. Predictably, the emphasis in understanding and treating these disorders, is on the development of a sense of personal efficacy, and much research is reported which substantiates this approach (further evidence of the extensive power of Bandura's efficacy theory). Because of space limitations, this review will not include the details of the research substantiating efficacy theory in clinical settings. Suffice it to say that personality disorders are seen as distortions of thinking. Accordingly, the most successful treatment consists of the acquisition of skills of thought that enable the individual to gain control of negative ruminative thoughts and replace them with thoughts that are optimistic, and in fact, usually more realistic. Bandura suggests teaching modeling and mastery skill. The Pacific Institute would add the skills of self-talk, visualization and affirmations.

Athletic Functioning

It is generally recognized that the way athletes think about themselves and their ability to perform under extremely tense conditions in highly competitive events actually influences their performances. Bandura has applied his efficacy theory to this important domain of human activity, and in so doing, he has stimulated much well-conceived research relating specifically to the relevance of perceived self-efficacy in such areas: development of athletic skills, self-regulation of athletic performance, collective team efficacy and psychobiological effects of physical exercise. This review will focus briefly on a few studies which capture the heart of Bandura's treatment of this topic, while at the same time provide the research support for some of the cognitive concepts we teach at The Pacific Institute.

Bandura and others show that cognitive simulation through visualization improves both development and performance of motor skills. Bandura explains that these skills were not as important as those produced by physical practice because of the "skimpy way in which they [visualization skills] are typically applied," and concludes that "athletes need efficacy-affirming evidence that they can exercise better control over their performance attainments with cognitive aids than without them."

In another study, Jourden and others demonstrated that subjects, who were instructed that performance of the assigned task was due to inherited ability, performed less effectively and experienced less development in perceived self-efficacy than another group of subjects who were told that they were essentially in control of their performance. The figure below shows this outcome graphically.

In a third study, Kane and others demonstrate the importance

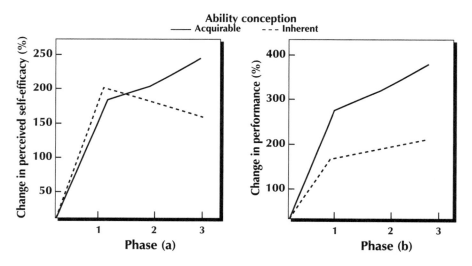

of perceived self-efficacy, particularly in highly competitive wrestling tournaments. In this study, the perceived self-efficacy, although important in the preliminary matches, was not as important in the final matches where the difference in physical abilities between the contestants was slight.

Bandura discusses factors that encourage collective team efficacy which is more than the aggregate of the individual efficacies of each team member. In a recent study by Hodge and Carron, one group of team members were given negative information about their physical strength, while another team was given favorable information about their strength. Actually, the two groups were comparable in strength. Quoting Hodges and Carron, "Teams whose collective efficacy was arbitrarily raised improved team's performance following competitive defeat. Teams whose sense of collective efficacy was lowered suffered substantial decrements in team performance."

Bandura cites evidence from Spinks' study that efficacy affects group processes and performance. "Teams with a strong sense of collective efficacy have high cohesiveness, whereas those of low collective efficacy experience more factionalism. On teams with high group cohesiveness, players subordinate their self-interests for team success and coordinate their efforts in deft teamwork. Among elite volleyball teams, players' beliefs in their teams' competitive efficacy, measured before the tournament, predicted their performance success in the contests."

Organizational Functioning/Collective Efficacy

Bandura chose to present collective efficacy in two components: Organizational Functioning and Collective Efficacy. In the former, considerable emphasis is given to two aspects of organizational functioning: Career development and mastery of occupational roles that are typically influenced more by personal rather than group efficacy. There are two other components to Bandura's discussion of Organizational Functioning that are both interesting and important: Self-Efficacy in Organizational Decision-Making and Collective Organizational Efficacy. The last chapter of Bandura's book is devoted to Collective Efficacy, and since this topic is of utmost importance and because of space limitations, most of this section of the review will focus on the collective efficacy chapter. Suffice it to say Bandura presents convincing evidence, from numerous studies, of the important role of efficacy in the selection and enactment of career decisions. (Here again, the power of his efficacy theory in this domain of human thought and action is substantiated.)

One final point before proceeding to the last chapter of Bandura's book. Bandura has an excellent treatment of the importance of self-efficacy in organizational decision-making. Essentially, he cites studies supporting the vital role of leaders' personal efficacy in the processes of decision-making in organizations. He laments the methodological difficulties of the studies that have been done. He, and others, devised an experiment that permitted the assessment of the importance of belief on the performance of all members of an organization. One group of individuals was told that the skills involved in the successful performance of carrying out the decisions in the study were inherent, while another group was told that the outcome of their efforts was essentially under their control. The latter group performed significantly better than the former, thus demonstrating the power of belief transmitted through a highly efficacious manager to other members of the organization, who in turn behaved in an efficacious manner.

In the words of Bandura, "Perceived collective efficacy is concerned with the performance capability of a social system as a whole. Belief in collective efficacy affects the sense of mission and purpose of a system, the strength of a common commitment to what it seeks to achieve, how well its members work together to produce results, and of the group's resiliency in the face of difficulties."

Collective Efficacy

Bandura defines collective efficacy as "a group's shared belief in its conjoint capabilities to organize and execute the course of action to produce given levels of attainment." Bandura stresses the importance of enabling (not empowering, a term that has "become meaningless through its use in promotional hype and political rhetoric"), in equipping people with a firm belief that they can produce valued effects by their collective action and in providing them with the means to do so." These are what Bandura says are the key ingredients in an enabling process. We at The Pacific Institute provide our clients with the means to become enablers.

Collective efficacy is not the algebraic sum of the individual efficacies of the members of an organization or group. "Importantly, personal and collective efficacy differ in the unit of agency, but in both forms efficacy beliefs have similar sources, serve similar functions, and operate through similar processes. These processes, which shared efficacy beliefs activate, affect how well group members work together and how much they accomplish collectively."

Bandura points to the methodological difficulties of measuring collective efficacy. Briefly, there are three ways of measuring collective efficacy: the aggregate of each member's self appraisal; the aggregate of each member's appraisal of how well their group performs as a whole; and a measure obtained by group members together. None of these approaches is perfect since the measures of collective efficacy obtained by all three methods would depend on a number of characteristics of the group being studied. For example, the degree of interdependence in the work style of the group may result in a measure of collective efficacy having spuriously lower predictability. Allowances can be made for these problems through careful analysis and statistical and experimental controls.

Bandura and others have shown that collective efficacy does indeed exist "as a group attribute," and that it predicts performance in many settings with many kinds of populations, including schools, organizations and athletic teams. Bandura concludes that, "The totality of teachers' beliefs in their own efficacy is just as predictive of school performance as the totality of teacher's beliefs in their schools' efficacy as a whole."

Bandura caps his magnum opus with an interesting discussion of the implications and applications of collective efficacy in the political and media domains. If people possess strong efficacy beliefs they are much more likely to be successful in their efforts to bring about political changes through social action. Some of these studies show the resiliency of politically efficacious people who seem to be more determined in bringing about social action as a result of initial failure.

Reading Bandura's most recent book strengthens my conviction that everything about Efficacy Theory is related to what we teach at The Pacific Institute. Bandura says, in effect, that having self or collective efficacy ENABLES people to do what they do better to work alone or as members of organizations in setting goals and to do so with greater persistence, resilience, creativity and with a higher probability of developing to their full potential. How much closer could this statement conform to our own mission statement?

About the Author

Albert Bandura is David Starr Jordan Professor of Social Science in Psychology at Stanford University and past President of the American Psychological Association. Among the awards he has received are the Distinguished Scientific Contribution Award of the American Psychological Association and the William James Award. He has been elected to the American Academy of Arts and Sciences and the Institute of Medicine of the National Academy of Sciences, and has received honorary degrees from eleven universities. He is the author of nine books, including, most recently, *Social Foundations of Thought and Action: A Social Cognitive Theory.* *(reprinted from book jacket)*

BIBLIOGRAPHY

Bennis, Warren, and Namus, Burt. *Leaders: The Strategy for Taking Charge.* New York, Harper and Row, 1985.

Bennis, Warren, *On Becoming a Leader,* Addison and Wesley, 1996.

Bryan, E.A., *Historical Sketch of the State College of Washington,* 1928, Alumni and the Associated Students.

Burns, J.M., "Leadership in American Politics", in Spilett, M.A. (ed) Proceedings of the Educational Leadership Conference, 1992, pp 10-15.

Clark, K.E. and Clark, M.B. *Choosing to Lead,* Second Edition. Center for Creative Leadership, 1996.

Clark, K.E. and Clark, M.B. (West Orange, N.J.) *Leadership Library of America* (1990).

Cohen, M.D. and March, J.D. *Leadership and Ambiguity: The American College President,* 1974, McGraw Hill.

Fry, Richard, *The Crimson and the Gray,* WSU Press, 1990.

Frykman, George, *Creating the People's University*, WSU Press, 1990

Gardner, John, Bell Atlantic Quarterly Vol 3, pages 49-60.

Hughes, Sally Campbell, "How to Tell Your Story." In Vitez, Michael, "There are No Rules For Writing Your Life Story." The Seattle Times, "There are No Rules for Writing Your Life Story." February, 2000.

Kennedy, Donald *John Gardner: A Salute*. Science, 22 March, 2002.

Landeen, W.M., *E.O.Holland and the State College of Washington*, 1958.

McGill, W.J., *The Year of the Monkey: Revolt on Campus 1968-69*. McGraw Hill, 1982.

Sample, Steven, *The Contrarian's Guide to Leadership*, Jossey-Bass, 2002.

Stimson, William, *Going to WSU: A Century of Student Life*, WSU Press, 1990.

Yammarino, F.J, and Bass, B.M. "Longterm Forecasting of Transformational Leadership and It's Effect Among Naval Officers." Some Preliminary Findings in Measurement of Leadership.(ed)